The KJV Dictionary

Uncommon, Doctrinal, & Thematic Terms
Defined by Noah Webster's 1828 Dictionary

Published by followers of Jesus Christ for
the promotion of the knowledge of God.

The KJV Dictionary

ISBN – 13: 978 – 0 – 615 – 35177 – 3

This book is available at discount pricing when ordered in quantities
or for educational purposes. Please reference the website below for
details.

Contact Information:
(734) 454 – 4449
www.KJVDictionary.com

Explanatory Notes

---

1. The classification of words has been noted as follows:

v. = verb
n. = noun
a. = adjective
adv. = adverb
pron. = pronoun
con. = connective
prep. = preposition
exclam. = exclamation

2. There were several words that could not be found in Noah's Webster's 1828 Dictionary. Rather than leave these important words out of The KJV Dictionary, these words were defined by Webster's 1913 Dictionary. If they could not be found in the 1913, they were defined by Strong's; these rare occurrences are noted next to each word as (1913) or (Strong's).

3. When Webster's Dictionary spells a word differently than the KJV Bible, the spelling of the KJV is retained. Example:

Webster's = 'Savior'
KJV Bible = 'Saviour'
The KJV Dictionary = 'Saviour'

4. Only definitions which apply to scripture are included.
Example: The word 'quail' has several meanings. However, only the biblical definition for 'quail' is used in The KJV Dictionary. The non-biblical definitions such as "to languish; to fail in spirits" are not included.

5. In most cases only the root word is defined. Example: Envied, Envies, Enviest, Envieth, and Envious are not defined; only the word 'Envy' is defined.

ABASE *v.*
To cast down; to reduce low; to depress; to humble; to degrade.

ABATED *v.*
Lessened; decreased; destroyed; mitigated; defeated; remitted; overthrown.

ABBA *n.*
In the Chaldee and Syriac, a father, and figuratively a superior.

ABHOR *v.*
1. To hate extremely, or with contempt; to lothe, detest or abominate.
2. To despise or neglect.
3. To cast off or reject.

ABIDE *v.*
1. To rest, or dwell.
2. To tarry or stay for a short time.
3. To continue permanently or in the same state; to be firm and immovable.
4. To wait for; to be prepared for; to await.
5. To bear or endure; to bear patiently.

ABJECT *n.*
A person in the lowest condition and despicable.

ABODE *n.*
1. Stay; continuance in a place; residence for a longer or shorter time.
2. A place of continuance; a dwelling; a habitation.
3. To make abode, to dwell or reside.

ABOLISH *v.*
1. To make void; to annul; to abrogate.
2. To destroy, or put an end to.

ABOMINABLE *a.*
1. Very hateful; detestable; lothesome.
2. Whatever is odious to the mind or offensive to the senses.
3. Unclean.

ABOMINATION *n.*
1. Extreme hatred; detestation.
2. The object of detestation.

ABROAD *adv.*
At large; widely; not confined to narrow limits.

ABSTAIN *v.*
To forbear, or refrain from,

voluntarily.

ABSTINENCE *n.*
1. The act or practice of voluntarily refraining from, or forbearing any action.
2. The refraining from an indulgence of appetite, or from customary gratifications of animal propensities.

ACCORD *n.*
1. Agreement; harmony of minds; consent or concurrence of opinions or wills.
2. Will; voluntary or spontaneous motion.

ACCURSE *v.*
To devote to destruction; to imprecate misery or evil upon.

ACQUAINT *v.*
1. To make known; to make fully or intimately known; to make familiar.
2. To inform; to communicate notice to.

ACQUIT *v.*
To set free; to release or discharge from an obligation, accusation, guilt, censure, suspicion, or what-ever lies upon a person as a charge or duty.

ADAMANT *n.*
A very hard or impenetrable stone.

ADDER *n.*
A venomous serpent or viper, of several species.

ADJURE *v.*
1. To charge, bind or command on oath, or under the penalty of a curse.
2. To charge earnestly and solemnly, on pain of God's wrath.
3. To conjure; to charge, urge or summon with solemnity.

ADMONISH *v.*
1. To warn or notify of a fault; to reprove with mildness.
2. To counsel against wrong practices; to caution or advise.
3. To instruct or direct.

ADMONITION *n.*
Gentle reproof; counseling against a fault; instruction in duties; caution; direction.

ADO *n.*
Bustle; trouble; labor; difficulty.

ADORN *v.*
1. To deck or decorate; to make beautiful; to add to beauty by dress; to deck with external ornaments.
2. To make pleasing, or more pleasing.
3. To display the beauty or excellence of.

ADORNING *v.*
Ornamenting; decorating; displaying beauty.

ADULTERY *n.*
1. Violation of the marriage bed; a crime, or a civil injury, which introduces, or may introduce, into a family, a spurious offspring.
2. All manner of lewdness or unchastity.
3. Idolatry, or apostasy from the true God.

ADVERSARY *n.*
1. An enemy or foe; one who has enmity at heart.
2. An opponent or antagonist.

ADVERSITY *n.*

An event, or series of events, which oppose success or desire; misfortune; calamity; affliction; distress; state of unhappiness.

ADVERTISE *v.*
To inform; to give notice, advice or intelligence to.

AFFINITY *n.*
1. The relation contracted by marriage, between a husband and his wife's kindred, and between a wife and her husband's kindred.
2. Agreement; relation; conformity; resemblance; connection.

AFORDING *v.*
Yielding; producing.

AFFRIGHTED *v.*
Suddenly alarmed with fear; terrified.

AFOOT *adv.*
1. On foot; borne by the feet; opposed to riding.
2. In action; in a state of being planned for execution.

AFORE *adv.*
1. In front.
2. Between one object and

another, so as to intercept a direct view or intercourse. **3.** Prior in time; before; anterior.

AFORETIME *adv.*
In time past; in a former time.

AFRESH *adv.*
Anew; again; recently; after intermission.

AGATE *n.*
A class of siliceous, semi-pellucid gems of many varieties, in various combinations, variegated with dots, zones, filaments, ramifications, arborizations, and various figures.

AGONE *v.*
Ago; past; since.

AGUE *n.*
1. The cold fit which precedes a fever, or a paroxysm of fever in intermittents.
2. Chilliness; a chill, or state of shaking with cold.

AIL *v.*
To trouble; to affect with uneasiness.

ALABASTER *n.*
A sub-variety of carbonate of lime, found in large masses, formed by the deposition of calcarious particles in caverns of limestone rocks.

ALAS *exclam.*
An exclamation expressive of sorrow, grief, pity, concern, or apprehension of evil.

ALBEIT
Be it so; admit all that; although; notwithstanding.

ALLEGE *v.*
To declare; to affirm; to assert; to pronounce with positiveness.

ALLEGORY *n.*
A figurative sentence or discourse, in which the principal subject is described by another subject resembling it in its properties and circumstances. The principal subject is thus kept out of view, and we are left to collect the intentions of the writer or speaker, by the resemblance of the secondary to the primary subject.

ALLELUIAH *n.*
Praise to Jehovah; a word
used to denote pious joy
and exultation.

ALLOW *v.*
To approve, justify, or
sanction.

ALLURE *v.*
To attempt to draw to; to
tempt by the offer of some
good, real or apparent; to
invite by something flatter-
ing or acceptable.

ALMS *n.*
Any thing given gratui-
tously to relieve the poor,
otherwise called charity.

ALMSDEED *n.*
An act of charity; a chari-
table gift.

ALOOF *adv.*
At a distance, but within
view, or at a small dis-
tance.

ALPHA *n.*
The first letter in the Greek
alphabet, answering to A,
and used to denote first or
beginning.

AMBASSAGE *n.*

An embassy.

AMEN *v.*
To confirm, establish, ver-
ify; to trust, or give confidence.

AMEND *v.*
1. To correct; to rectify by
expunging a mistake.
2. To reform, by quitting
bad habits; to make better
in a moral sense.
3. To grow or become better, by reformation, or rec-
tifying something wrong in
manners or morals.

AMENDS *n.*
Compensation for an in-
jury; recompense; satisfaction; equivalent.

AMERCE *v.*
To inflict a penalty at
mercy; to punish by a pe-
cuniary penalty.

AMIABLE *a.*
Lovely; worth of love; deserving of affection.

AMISS *a.*
1. Wrong; faulty; out of
order; improper.
2. In a faulty manner; contrary to propriety, truth,

law or morality.

ANATHEMA *n.*
Excommunication with
curses.

ANGLE *n.*
A hook; an instrument to
take fish, consisting of a
rod, a line and a hook, or a
line and hook.

ANGUISH *n.*
Extreme pain, either of
body or mind.

ANOINT *v.*
1. To pour oil upon; to
smear or rub over with oil
or unctuous substances;
also to spread over, as oil.
2. To consecrate by unction, or the use of oil.
3. To smear or daub.

ANON *adv.*
1. Quickly; without intermission: soon; immedi-
ately.
2. Sometimes; now and
then; at other times.

ANTICHRIST *n.*
A great adversary of
Christ; the man of sin.

ANTIQUITY *n.*

Ancientness; great age; the
quality of being ancient.

ANVIL *n.*
An iron block with a
smooth face, on which
smiths hammer and shape
their work.

APACE *adv.*
With a quick pace; quick;
fast; speedily; with haste;
hastily.

APOSTLE *n.*
A person deputed to exe-
cute some important busi-
ness; a disciple of Christ
commissioned to preach
the gospel.

APOTHECARY *n.*
One who practices phar-
macy; one who prepares
drugs for medicinal uses,
and keeps them for sale.

APPAREL *n.*
Clothing; vesture; gar-
ments; dress.

APPEAL *v.*
To refer to a superior judge
or court, for the decision of
a cause depending, or the
revision of a cause decided
in a lower court.

APPEASE *v.*
To make quiet; to calm; to reduce to a state of peace; to still; to pacify.

APPERTAIN *v.*
To belong, whether by right, nature or appointment.

APPREHEND *v.*
1. To take or seize; to take hold of.
2. To take with the understanding, to conceive in the mine; to understand, without passing a judgment, or making an inference.

APT *a.*
1. Fit; suitable.
2. Qualified.

ARCHANGEL *n.*
An angel of the highest order; an angel occupying the eighth rank in the celestial hierarchy.

ARCTURUS *n.*
A fixed star of the first magnitude, in the constellation of Bootes.

ARIGHT *adv.*
Rightly; in a right form; without mistake or crime.

ARK *n.*
1. A small close vessel, chest or coffer.
2. The large floating vessel, in which Noah and his family were preserved, during the deluge.
3. A depository.

ARMHOLE *n.*
A hole for the arm in a garment.

ARRAY *n.*
1. Order; disposition in regular lines.
2. Dress; garments disposed in order upon the person.

ARRAY *v.*
1. To place or dispose in order.
2. To deck or dress; to adorn with dress.

ART
The second person, indicative mode, present tense, of the substantive verb am.

ASCEND *v.*
To move upwards; to mount; to go up; to rise.

ASCENT *n.*
1. The way by which one

ascends; the means of ascending.
2. An eminence, hill or high place.

ASP *n.*
A small poisonous serpent of Egypt and Libya, whose bite occasions inevitable death, but without pain.

ASS *n.*
A quadruped of the equine genus. This animal has long slouching ears, a short mane, and a tail covered with long hairs at the end.

ASSAY *v.*
To attempt, try or endeavor.

ASSENT *n.*
Accord; agreement.

ASSENT *v.*
To admit as true; to agree, yield or concede; to express an agreement of the mind to what is alleged, or proposed.

ASSWAGE *v.*
1. To soften; to allay, mitigate, ease or lessen; to appease or pacify.
2. To abate or subside.

ASTONIED *v.*
Amazed; confounded with fear, surprise, or admiration.

ASUNDER *adv.*
Apart; into parts; separately; in a divided state.

ATHIRST *a.*
Thirsty; wanting drink.

ATONEMENT *n.*
1. Agreement; concord; reconciliation, after enmity or controversy.
2. Expiation; satisfaction or reparation made by giving an equivalent for an injury, or by doing or suffering that which is received in satisfaction for an offense or injury.
3. The expiation of sin made by the obedience and personal sufferings of Christ.

ATTAIN *v.*
1. To reach; to come to or arrive at, by motion, bodily exertion, or efforts towards a place or object.
2. To reach; to come to or arrive at, by an effort of mind.

ATTENT *a.*
Attentive.

AUL *n.*
An iron instrument for piercing small holes in leather, for sewing and stitching; used by shoemakers, sadlers, &c.

AUSTERE *a.*
Severe; harsh; rigid; stern.

AVAIL *v.*
1. To profit one's self; to turn to advantage.
2. To assist or profit; to effect the object, or bring to a successful issue.

AVENGED *v.*
Satisfied by the punishment of the offender; vindicated; punished.

AVERSE *a.*
1. Disliking; unwilling; having a repugnance of mind.
2. Unfavorable; indisposed; malign.

AVOUCH *v.*
1. To affirm; to declare or assert with positiveness.
2. To produce or call in; to affirm in favor of, maintain or support.

AXLETREE *n.*
A piece of timer or bar of iron, fitted for insertion in the hobs or naves of wheels, on which the wheels turn.

BAAL *n.*
An idol among the ancient Chaldeans and Syrians, representing the sun.

BACKBITE *v.*
To censure, slander, reproach, or speak evil of the absent.

BACKSLIDE *v.*
To fall off; to apostatize.

BADE *past tense of bid.*

BAKEMEATS *n.*
Meats prepared for food in an oven.

BALM *n.*
1. The sap or juice of trees or shrubs remarkably odoriferous or aromatic.
2. Any fragrant or valuable ointment.
3. Anything which heals, or which soothes or mitigates pain.

BANISH *v.*
To condemn to exile, or compel to leave one's country, by authority of the prince or government, either for life or for a limited time.

BANQUETING *v.*
Feasting; entertaining with rich fare.

BAPTISM *n.*
1. The application of water to a person.
2. The sufferings of Christ.

BARBARIAN *n.*
A man in his rude, savage state; an uncivilized person.

BARREN *a.*
1. Not producing young, or offspring.
2. Not producing plants; unfruitful; steril; not fertile; producing little; unproductive.
3. Not producing the usual fruit.

BASE *a.*
1. Low in place.
2. Mean; vile; worthless; low in value or estimation.
3. Of low station; of mean account; without rank, dignity or estimation among men.

BASON *n.*
A hollow vessel or dish, to hold water for washing, and for various other uses.

BASTARD *n.*
A natural child; a child begotten and born out of wedlock; an illegitimate or spurious child.

BATH *n.*
A Hebrew measure containing the tenth of a homer, or seven gallons and four pints, as a measure for liquids; and three pecks and three pints, as a dry measure.

BATTERED *v.*
Beaten; bruised, broken, impaired by beating or wearing.

BATTLEMENT *n.*
A wall raised on a building with openings or embrasures, or the embrasure itself.

BAY *a.*
Red, or reddish, inclining

to a chestnut color.

BAY *n.*
1. An arm of the sea, extending into the land, not of any definite form, but smaller than a gulf, and larger than a creek.
2. The laurel tree.

BEACON *n.*
Figuratively, that which gives notice of danger.

BEAR *v.*
To support; to sustain.

BECKON *v.*
To make a sign to another, by nodding, winking, or a motion of the hand or finger.

BEDSTEAD *n.*
A frame for supporting a bed.

BEEVES *n.*
Cattle; quadrupeds of the bovine genus.

BEFALL *v.*
To happen to; to occur to.

BEGAT *v.*
To procreate; to generate.

BEGET *v.*
To procreate; to generate.

BEGOTTEN *v.*
Procreated; generated.

BEGUILE *v.*
To delude; to deceive; to impose on by artifice or craft.

BEHEMOTH *n.*
A beast or brute.

BEHOLD *v.*
To fix the eyes upon; to see with attention; to observe with care.

BEHOVE *v.*
To be necessary for; to be fit for; to be meet for, with respect to necessity, duty, or convenience.

BELIAL *n.*
Unprofitableness; wickedness.

BELIE *v.*
To give the lie to; to show to be false; to charge with falsehood.

BELLOW *v.*
To make a hollow, loud noise.

BEMOAN *v.*
To lament; to bewail; to
express sorrow for.

BEREAVE *v.*
1. To deprive; to strip; to
make destitute.
2. To take away from.

BERYL *n.*
A mineral.

BESEECH *v.*
To entreat; to supplicate; to
implore; to ask or pray
with urgency.

BESET *v.*
1. To surround; to inclose;
to hem in; to besiege.
2. To press on all sides; to
entangle.

BESIEGE *v.*
1. To lay siege to; to beleaguer; to beset, or surround
with armed forces, for the
purpose of compelling to
surrender, either by famine
or by violent attacks.
2. To beset; to throng
round.

BESOM *n.*
A broom; a brush of twigs
for sweeping.

BESOUGHT *v.*
Entreated; implored;
sought by entreaty.

BESTEAD *v.*
1. To accommodate.
2. To dispose.

BESTIR *v.*
To put into brisk or vigorous action; to move with
life and vigor.

BESTOWED *v.*
Given gratuitously; con-
ferred; laid out; applied;
deposited for safe-keeping.

BETHINK *v.*
To call to mind; to recall or
bring to recollection, re-
flection, or consideration.

BETIMES *adv.*
Seasonably; in good sea-
son or time; before it is
late.

BETRAY *v.*
1. To deliver into the
hands of an enemy by
treachery or fraud, in violation of trust.
2. To violate by fraud, or
unfaithfulness.
3. To violate confidence
by disclosing a secret, or

that which was intrusted; to expose.

BETROTH *v.*
1. To contract to any one, in order to a future marriage; to promise or pledge one to be the future spouse of another.
2. To contract with one for a future spouse; to espouse.

BETWIXT *prep.*
1. Between; in the space that separates two persons or things.
2. Passing between; from one to another, noting intercourse.

BEWRAY *v.*
To disclose perfidiously; to betray; to show or make visible.

BID *v.*
1. To ask; to request; to invite.
2. To command; to order or direct.
3. To proclaim; to make known by a public voice.
4. To pronounce or declare.
5. To wish or pray.

BIER *n.*
A carriage or frame of wood for conveying dead human bodies to the grave.

BILLOW *n.*
A great wave or surge of the sea, occasioned usually by violent wind.

BIND *v.*
1. To tie together, or confine with a cord, or any thing that is flexible; to fasten.
2. To confine or restrain, as with a chain, fetters or cord.
3. To oblige by a promise, vow, stipulation, covenant, law, duty or any other moral tie; to engage.
4. To confirm or ratify.

BISHOP *n.*
An overseer; a spiritual superintendent, ruler or director.

BISHOPRICK *n.*
The charge of instructing and governing in spiritual concerns; office.

BLAIN *n.*
A pustule; a botch; a blister.

BLASPHEME *v.*
To speak of the Supreme
Being in terms of impious
irreverence; to revile or
speak reproachfully of
God, or the Holy Spirit.

BLEATING *n.*
The cry of a sheep.

BLEMISH *v.*
1. Too mark with any deformity; to injure or impair
any thing which is well
formed, or excellent; to
mar, or make defective,
either the body or mind.
2. To tarnish, as reputation
or character; to defame.

BLEMISH *n.*
Any mark of deformity;
any scar or defect that di-
minishes beauty, or renders
imperfect that which is
well formed.

BLESS *v.*
1. To pronounce a wish of
happiness to one; to ex-
press a wish or desire of
happiness.
2. To make happy; to make
successful; to prosper in
temporal concerns.
3. To make happy in a future life.

4. To set apart or consecrate to holy purposes; to
make and pronounce holy.
5. To consecrate by prayer;
to invoke a blessing upon.
6. To praise; to glorify, for
benefits received.

BLOW *n.*
1. The act of striking; more
generally the stroke; a violent application of the
hand, fist, or an instrument
to an object.
2. The fatal stroke; a stroke
that kills.
3. An act of hostility.
4. A sudden calamity; a
sudden or severe evil.
5. A single act; a sudden
event.

BLOSSOM *v.*
To flourish and prosper.

BOIL *n.*
A tumor upon the flesh,
accompanied with soreness
and inflammation; a sore
angry swelling.

BOISTEROUS *a.*
1. Loud; roaring; violent;
stormy.
2. Turbulent; furious; tumultuous; noisy.
3. Large; unwieldy; huge;

clumsily violent.
4. Violent.

BOLL *v.*
To form into a pericarp or seed-vessel.

BOLSTER *n.*
A long pillow or cushion, used to support the head of persons lying on a bed.

BONDAGE *n.*
1. Obligation; tie of duty.
2. Spiritual subjection to sin and corrupt passions, or to the yoke of the ceremonial law; servile fear.

BONDMAID *n.*
A female slave, or one bound to service without wages, in opposition to a hired servant.

BONDMAN *n.*
A man slave, or one bound to service without wages.

BOND *a.*
In a state of servitude, or slavery; captive.

BONDSERVANT *n.*
A slave; one who is subjected to the authority of another, or whose person

and liberty are restrained.

BONDSERVICE *n.*
The condition of a bondservant; slavery.

BONDWOMAN *n.*
A woman slave.

BONNET *n.*
A covering for the head.

BOOTY *n.*
1. Spoil taken from an enemy in war; plunder; pillage.
2. That which is seized by violence and robbery.

BORNE *v.*
Carried; conveyed; supported; defrayed.

BOSOM *n.*
1. Embrace, as with the arms; inclosure; compass.
2. The breast, or its interior, considered as a close place, the receptacle of secrets.
3. The tender affections; kindness; favor.
4. The arms, or embrace of the arms.

BOSS *n.*
A stud or knob: a protuber-

ant ornament.

BOTCH *n.*
A swelling on the skin; a large ulcerous affection.

BOUGH *n.*
The branch of a tree.

BOUND *v.*
To limit; to terminate; to fix the furthest point of extension.

BOUNTIFUL *a.*
Free to give; liberal in bestowing gifts and favors; munificent; generous.

BOUNTY *n.*
Liberality in bestowing gifts and favors; generosity; munificence.

BOW *v.*
1. To bend; to inflect.
2. To bend the body in token of respect or civility.
3. To bend or incline towards, in condescension.

BOW *n.*
Bow of a ship, is the rounding part of her side forward, beginning where the planks arch inwards, and terminating where they close, at the stem or prow.

BOWELS *n.*
1. The intestines of an animal; the entrails, especially of man. The heart.
2. The interior part of any thing.
3. The seat of pity or kindness.

BRAMBLE *n.*
The raspberry bush or blackberry bush.

BRAND *n.*
A burning piece of wood; a stick or piece of wood partly burnt.

BRANDISH *v.*
To move or wave; to raise, and move in various directions; to shake or flourish.

BRASEN *a.*
Made of brass.

BRAVERY *n.*
1. Courage; heroism; undaunted spirit; intrepidity; gallantry; fearlessness of danger.
2. Splendor; magnificence; showy appearance.

BRAWL *v.*

1. To quarrel noisily and indecently.
2. To speak loud and indecently.

BRAY *v.*
To pound, beat or grind small.

BRAY *n.*
The harsh sound or roar of an ass; a harsh grating sound.

BREACH *n.*
1. The act of breaking; or state of being broken; a rupture; a break; a gap.
2. The violation of a law; the violation or non-fulfillment of a contract; the non-performance of a moral duty.
3. Infraction; injury; invasion.

BRED *v.*
Generated; produced; contrived; educated.

BREECHES *n.*
A garment worn by men, covering the hips and thighs.

BRETHREN *plural of brother.*

BRIBE *v.*
To give or promise a reward or consideration, with a view to pervert the judgment, or corrupt the conduct. To hire for bad purposes; to purchase the decision of a judge, the testimony of a witness, or the performance of some act contrary to known truth, justice or rectitude.

BRIDLE *v.*
To restrain, guide or govern; to check, curb or control.

BRIER *n.*
A prickly plant or shrub.

BRIGANDINE *n.*
A coat of mail.

BRIM *n.*
The rim, lip or broadborder of any vessel or other thing.

BRIMSTONY *a.*
Full of brimstone, or containing it; resembling brimstone; sulphurous.

BRINK *n.*
The edge, margin or border of a steep place.

BROAD *a.*
Wide; extended in breadth, or from side to side.

BROID *v.*
To braid.

BROIDER *v.*
To adorn with figures of needle work.

BROIL *v.*
To agitate with heat; to dress or cook over coals, before the fire.

BROOD *n.*
A hatch; the young birds hatched at once.

BROOK *n.*
A small natural stream of water, or a current flowing from a spring or fountain less than a river.

BROTH *n.*
Liquor in which flesh is boiled and macerated.

BROW *n.*
1. The prominent ridge over the eye, forming an arch above the orbit.
2. The edge of a steep place.

BRUIT *n.*
Report; rumor; fame.

BRUTE *a.*
Senseless; unconscious.

BRUTISH *a.*
Insensible; stupid.

BUCKLER *n.*
A kind of shield, or piece of defensive armor.

BUFFET *v.*
To strike with the hand or fist; to box; to beat.

BULLOCK *n.*
An ox, or castrated bull.

BULRUSH *n.*
A large kind of rush, growing in wet land or water, and without knots.

BULWARK *n.*
1. In fortification, a bastion, or a rampart; a mound of earth round a place, capable of resisting cannon shot, and formed with bastions, curtains, &c.
2. A fortification; any means of defense.
3. That which secures against an enemy or external annoyance; a screen or

shelter; means of protection and safety.

BUSHEL *n.*
A dry measure, containing eight gallons, or four pecks.

BUSYBODY *n.*
A meddling person; one who officiously concerns himself with the affairs of others.

BUTLER *n.*
A servant or officer in the houses of princes and great men, whose principal business is to take charge of the liquors, place, &c.

BUTTOCK *n.*
The rump, or the protuberant part behind.

BYWAY *n.*
A secluded, private or obscure way.

BYWORD *n.*
A common saying; a proverb; a saying that has a general currency.

CAB *n.*
An oriental dry measure, being the sixth part of a

seah or satum, and the eighteenth of an ephah; containing two pints and five sixths English and American corn measure.

CALAMITY *n.*
Any great misfortune, or cause of misery.

CALDRON *n.*
A large kettle or boiler, of copper, or other metal, furnished with a movable handle or bail, with which to hang it on a chimney hook.

CALKER *n.*
A man who calks; a calk or pointed iron on a house-shoe.

CANDLE-STICK *n.*
An instrument or utensil to hold a candle, made in different forms and of different materials; a stick or piece of wood.

CANKER *n.*
A virulent, corroding ulcer; any thing that corrodes, corrupts or destroys.

CARBUNCLED *a.*
Set with carbuncles; spot-

ted.

CARCASS *n.*
The body of an animal.

CARNAL *a.*
1. Pertaining to flesh;
fleshly; sensual.
2. Being in the natural
state; unregenerate.
3. Pertaining to the ceremonial law.
4. Lecherous; lustful; libidinous; given to sensual
indulgence.

CARRIAGE *n.*
That which carries; a vehicle.

CASEMENT *n.*
A little movable window,
usually within a large,
made to turn and open on
hinges.

CAST *v.*
1. To throw, fling or send.
2. To throw, to extend.

CASTAWAY *n.*
That which is thrown
away. A person abandoned
by God, as unworthy of his
favor; a reprobate.

CAUL *n.*
A membrane in the abdo-
men, covering the greatest
part of the lower intestines.

CEASE *v.*
1. To stop moving, acting
or speaking; to leave of; to
give over.
2. To stop; to be at an end.
3. To abstain.
4. To put a stop to; to put
an end to.

CELESTIAL *a.*
1. Heavenly; belonging or
relating to heaven; dwelling in heaven.
2. Belonging to the upper
regions, or visible heaven.
3. Descending from
heaven.

CELLAR *n.*
A room under a house or
other building.

CENSER *n.*
A vase or pan in which incense is burned.

CENTURION *n.*
A military officer who
commanded a hundred
men, a century or company
of infantry, answering to
the captain in modern ar-
mies.

CHAFED *v.*
Heated or fretted by rubbing; worn by friction.

CHAMBER *n.*
1. An apartment in an upper story, or in a story above the lower floor of a dwelling house.
2. Any retired room; any private apartment which a person occupies.
3. Any retired place.

CHAMBERING *n.*
Wanton, lewd, immodest behavior.

CHAMBERLAIN *n.*
An officer charged with the direction and management of a chamber, or of chambers.

CHAMOIS *n.*
An animal of the goat kind, whose skin is made into soft leather, called shammy.

CHAMPAIGN *n.*
A flat open country.

CHANT *v.*
To sing; to utter a melodious voice; to cant or throw the voice in modulations.

CHAPITER *n.*
The upper part or capital of a column or pillar.

CHARGED *v.*
Loaded; burdened; attacked; laid on; instructed; imputed; accused; placed to the debt; ordered; commanded.

CHARGER *n.*
A large dish.

CHARIOT *n.*
A car or vehicle.

CHARITY *n.*
1. Love, benevolence, good will.
2. Candor; liberality in judging of men and their actions; a disposition which inclines men to think and judge favorably, and to put the best construction on words and actions which the case will admit.

CHASTE *a.*
1. Pure from all unlawful commerce of sexes.
2. Free from obscenity.
3. Pure; genuine; uncorrupt; free from barbarous words and phrases, and

from quaint, affected, extravagant expressions.

CHASTEN *v.*
To correct by punishment; to punish; to inflict pain for the purpose of reclaiming an offender.

CHASTISE *v.*
To correct by punishing; to punish; to inflict pain by stripes, or in other manner, for the purpose of punishing an offender and recalling him to his duty.

CHATTER *v.*
To utter sounds rapidly and indistinctly.

CHEMARIMS *n.*
(Strongs)
Idolatrous priests.

CHERISH *v.*
1. To treat with tenderness and affection; to give warmth, ease or comfort to.
2. To hold as dear; to embrace with affection; to foster, and encourage.
3. To harbor; to indulge and encourage in the mind.

CHERUB *n.*

A figure composed of various creatures.

CHIDE *v.*
1. To scold at; to reprove; to utter words in anger, or by way of disapprobation; to rebuke.
2. To blame; to reproach.

CHRIST *n.*
The Anointed; an appellation given to the Savior of the World, and synonymous with the Hebrew Messiah.

CHRISTIAN *n.*
The name first given at Antioch to Christ's followers.

CHRONICLES *n.*
Hebrew "Words" or "Acts of days."

CHURCH *n.*
An organized body, whose unity does not depend on its being met together in one place; not an assemblage of atoms, but members in their several places united to the One Head, Christ, and forming one organic living whole; The bride of Christ; The house-

hold of Christ and of God;
The temple of the Holy
Spirit.

CHURL *n.*
1. A rude, surly, ill-bred
man.
2. A rustic; a countryman,
or laborer.
3. A miser.

CHURNING *n.*
The operation of making
butter from cream by agitation; a shaking or stirring.

CIELED *v.*
Overlaid with timber, or
with plastering.

CIRCUMCISE *v.*
To cut off the prepuce or
foreskin of males.

CIRCUMSPECT *a.*
Looking on all sides; looking round.

CISTERN *n.*
1. An artificial reservoir or
receptacle for holding water, beer or other liquor.
2. A natural reservoir; a
hollow place containing
water.

CLAD *v.*

Clothed; invested; covered
as with a garment.

CLAMOROUS *a.*
Speaking and repeating
loud words; noisy; vocifer-
ous; loud; turbulent.

CLAMOUR *n.*
A great outcry; noise; exclamation; vociferation,
made by a loud human
voice continued or re-
peated, or by a multitude
of voices.

CLAVE *past tense of
cleave.*

CLEAVE *v.*
1. To stick; to adhere; to
hold to.
2. To unite aptly; to fit; to
sit well on.
3. To part or divide by
force; to split or rive; to
open or sever the cohering
parts of a body, by cutting
or by the application of
force.
4. To part or open natu-
rally.

CLEFT *v.*
Divided; split; parted asunder.

CLEFT *n.*
A space or opening made by splitting; a crack; a crevice.

CLIFTED *a.*
Broken.

CLOD *n.*
A hard lump of earth, of any kind.

CLOKE *n.*
A loose outer garment worn over other clothes both by men and women.

CLOKE *v.*
To hide; to conceal; to use a false covering.

CLOUT *n.*
1. A patch; a piece of cloth or leather, &c., to close a breach.
2. A piece of cloth for mean purposes.

CLOUT *v.*
To patch; to mend by sewing on a piece or patch.

CLOVEN *v.*
Divided; parted.

CLUSTER *n.*
1. A bunch; a number of things of the same kind growing or joined together; a knot.
2. A number of individuals or things collected or gathered into a close body.

COCK *n.*
The male of birds.

COCKATRICE *n.*
A serpent imagined to proceed from a cocks egg.

COCKLE *n.*
A plant or weed that grows among corn.

COFFER *n.*
1. A chest or trunk.
2. A chest of money; a treasure.

COGITATION *n.*
1. The act of thinking; thought; meditation; contemplation.
2. Thought directed to an object; purpose.

COLLEGE *n.*
1. A collection, assemblage or society of men, invested with certain powers and rights, performing certain duties, or engaged in some common employ-

ment, or pursuit.

2. An assembly for a political or ecclesiastical purpose.

COLLOP *n.*
A small slice of meat; a piece of flesh.

COMELY *a.*
1. Properly, becoming; suitable: whence, handsome; graceful.
2. Decent; suitable; proper; becoming; suited to time, place, circumstances or persons.

COMMEND *v.*
1. To represent as worthy of notice, regard, or kindness; to speak in favor of; to recommend.
2. To commit; to entrust or give in charge.
3. To make acceptable or more acceptable.
4. To produce or present to favorable notice.

COMMENDATION *n.*
Ground of esteem, approbation or praise; that which presents a person or thing to another in a favorable light, and renders worthy of regard, or acceptance.

COMMISSION *n.*
Charge; order; mandate; authority given.

COMMIT *v.*
1. To give in trust; to put into the hands or power of another; to entrust.
2. To do; to effect or perpetrate.

COMMOTION *n.*
Tumult of people; disturbance; disorder.

COMMUNE *v.*
1. To converse; to talk together familiarly; to impart sentiments mutually, in private or familiar discourse.
2. To have intercourse in contemplation or meditation.

COMMUNICATE *v.*
To impart; to give to another; to confer for joint possession; to bestow.

COMMUNION *n.*
Fellowship; intercourse between two persons or more; interchange of transactions, or offices; a state of giving and receiving; agreement; concord.

COMPASS *n.*
1. Stretch; reach; extent; the limit or boundary of a space, and the space included.
2. A passing round; a circular course; a circuit.
3. Moderate bounds; limits of truth; moderation; due limits.

COMPASS *v.*
1. To stretch round; to extend so as to embrace the whole.
2. To surround; to environ; to inclose on all sides.
3. To go or walk round.
4. To besiege; to beleaguer; to block up.
5. To obtain; to attain to; to procure; to bring within ones power; to accomplish.

COMPASSION *n.*
A suffering with another; painful sympathy; a sensation of sorrow excited by the distress or misfortunes of another; pity; commiseration.

COMPEL *v.*
To drive or urge with force, or irresistibly; to constrain; to oblige; to necessitate, either by physical or moral force.

COMPOSITION *n.*
The state of being placed together; union; conjunction; combination.

CONCEAL *v.*
1. To keep close or secret; to forbear to disclose; to withhold from utterance or declaration.
2. To hide; to withdraw from observation; to cover or keep from sight.

CONCEIT *n.*
Conception; that which is conceived, imagined, or formed in the mind; idea; thought; image.

CONCEIVE *v.*
1. To receive into the womb, and breed; to begin the formation of the embryo or fetus of animal.
2. To form in the mind; to imagine; to devise.
3. To form an idea in the mind; to understand; to comprehend.
4. To understand; to comprehend; to have a complete idea of.

CONCEPTION *n.*

1. The act of conceiving; the first formation of the embryo or fetus of an animal.
2. Apprehension; knowledge.

CONCISION *n.*
A cutting off.

CONCLUDED *v.*
Shut; ended; finished; determined; inferred; comprehended; stopped, or bound.

CONCORD *n.*
Agreement between persons; union in opinions, sentiments, views or interests; peace; harmony.

CONCOURSE *n.*
A meeting; an assembly of men; an assemblage of things; a collection formed by a voluntary or spontaneous moving and meeting in one place.

CONCUBINE *n.*
A wife of inferior condition; a lawful wife, but not united to the man by the usual ceremonies, and of inferior condition.

CONCUPISCENCE *n.*
Lust; unlawful or irregular desire of sexual pleasure.

CONDEMN *v.*
1. To pronounce to be utterly wrong; to utter a sentence of disapprobation against; to censure; to blame.
2. To determine or judge to be wrong, or guilty; to disallow; to disapprove.
3. To witness against; to show or prove to be wrong, or guilty, by a contrary practice.
4. To pronounce to be guilty; to sentence to punishment; to utter sentence against judicially; to doom.

CONDESCEND *v.*
1. To descend from the privileges of superior rank or dignity, to do some act to an inferior, which strict justice or the ordinary rules of civility do not require.
2. To stoop or descend; to yield; to submit.

CONDUIT *n.*
A canal or pipe for the conveyance of water; an aqueduct.

CONEY *n.*
A rabbit; a quadruped of the genus Lepus, which has a short tail and naked ears.

CONFECTION *n.*
A composition or mixture.

CONFEDERACY *n.*
A league, or covenant; a contract between two or more persons, bodies of men or states, combined in support of each other, in some act or enterprise; mutual engagement; federal compact.

CONFEDERATE *a.*
United in a league; allied by treaty; engaged in a confederacy.

CONFER *v.*
1. To discourse; to converse; to consult together.
2. To compare; to examine by comparison.

CONFESS *v.*
1. To own, acknowledge or avow.
2. To own, avow or acknowledge; publicly to declare a belief in and adherence to.
3. To own and acknowledge.
4. To own; to acknowledge; to declare to be true, or to admit or assent to in words.

CONFOUND *v.*
1. To mix or blend, so as to occasion a mistake of one thing for another.
2. To perplex; to disturb the apprehension by indistinctness of ideas or words.
3. To abash; to throw the mind into disorder; to cast down; to make ashamed.
4. To perplex with terror; to terrify; to dismay; to astonish; to throw into consternation; to stupify with amazement.

CONGEAL *v.*
To change from a fluid to a solid sate; to harden into ice, or into a substance of less solidity.

CONGREGATION *n.*
1. The act of bringing together, or assembling.
2. An assembly or persons.
3. An assembly of rulers.

CONSCIENCE *n.*
Internal or self-knowledge,

or judgment of right and wrong; the faculty, power or principle within us, which decides on the lawfulness or unlawfulness of our own actions and affections, and instantly approves or condemns them.

CONSECRATE *v.*
To make or declare to be sacred, by certain ceremonies or rites; to appropriate to sacred uses; to set apart, dedicate, or devote, to the service and worship of God.

CONSENT *n.*
1. Agreement of the mind to what is proposed or state by another; accord; a yielding of the mind or will to that which is proposed.
2. Accord of minds; agreement; unity of opinion.
3. Agreement; coherence; correspondence in parts, qualities, or operation.

CONSOLATION *n.*
1. Comfort; alleviation of misery, or distress of mind; refreshment of mind or spirits; a comparative degree of happiness in distress or misfortune, spring-ing from any circumstance that abates the evil, or supports and strengthens the mind.
2. That which comforts, or refreshes the spirits; the cause of comfort.

CONSORT *v.*
To associate; to unite in company; to keep company.

CONSPIRACY *n.*
A combination of men for an evil purpose; an agreement between two or more persons, to commit some crime in concert.

CONSPIRATOR *n.*
One who conspires; one who engages in a plot to commit a crime.

CONSPIRE *v.*
To agree, by oath, covenant or otherwise, to commit a crime; to plot; to hatch treason.

CONSTRAIN *v.*
To strain; to press; to urge; to drive; to exert force, physical or moral, either in urging to action or in restraining it.

CONSULTATION *n.*
The act of consulting; deliberation of two or more persons, with a view to some decision.

CONSUME *v.*
1. To destroy, by separating the parts of a thing, by decomposition, devouring, and annihilating the form of a substance.
2. To destroy by dissipating or by use; to expend; to waste; to squander.
3. To spend; to cause to pass away, as time.
4. To cause to disappear; to waste slowly.
5. To destroy; to bring to utter ruin; to exterminate.

CONSUMMATION *n.*
Completion; end; perfection of a word, process or scheme.

CONSUMPTION *n.*
The act of consuming; waste; destruction by burning, eating, devouring, scattering, dissipation, slow decay, or by passing away.

CONTEMN *v.*
1. To despise; to consider and treat as mean and despicable; to scorn.
2. To slight; to neglect as unworthy of regard; to reject with disdain.

CONTEMPT *n.*
1. The act of despising; the act of viewing or considering and treating as mean, vile and worthless; disdain; hatred of what is mean or deemed vile.
2. The state of being despised.

CONTEMPTIBLE *a.*
Worthy of contempt; that deserves scorn, or disdain; despicable; mean; vile.

CONTEMPTUOUSLY *adv.*
In a contemptuous manner; with scorn or disdain; despitefully.

CONTEND *v.*
1. To strive, or to strive against; to struggle in opposition.
2. To strive; to use earnest efforts to obtain, or to defend and preserve.
3. To dispute earnestly; to strive in debate.
4. To reprove sharply; to chide; to strive to convince

and reclaim.

5. To strive in opposition; to punish.

6. To quarrel; to dispute fiercely; to wrangle.

CONTENT *a.*
Quiet; not disturbed; having a mind at peace; easy; satisfied, so as not to repine, object, or oppose.

CONTENTION *n.*
1. Strife; struggle; a violent effort to obtain something, or to resist a person, claim or injury; contest; quarrel.

2. Strife in words or debate; quarrel; angry contest; controversy.

3. Strife or endeavor to excel; emulation.

CONTENTIOUS *a.*
1. Apt to contend; given to angry debate; quarrelsome; perverse.

2. Exciting or adapted to provoke contention or disputes.

CONTRARIWISE *adv.*
On the contrary; oppositely; on the other hand.

CONTRARY *a.*

1. Opposite; adverse; moving against or in an opposite direction.

2. Contradictory; not merely different, but inconsistent or repugnant.

CONTRITE *a.*
Broken-hearted for sin; deeply affected with grief and sorrow for having offended God; humble; penitent.

CONTROVERSY *n.*
1. Dispute; debate; agitation of contrary opinions.

2. A suit in law; a case in which opposing parties contend for their respective claims before a tribunal.

3. Dispute; opposition carried on.

4. Opposition; resistance.

CONVENIENT *a.*
Fit; suitable; proper; adapted to use or to wants; commodious.

CONVERSATION *n.*
General course of manners; behavior; deportment.

CONVERT *v.*
To turn or be changed; to

undergo a change.

CONVEY *v.*
1. To carry, bear or transport.
2. To pass or cause to pass; to transmit.

CONVICT *v.*
1. To determine the truth of a charge against one; to prove or find guilty of a crime charged; to determine or decide to be guilty.
2. To convince of sin; to prove or determine to be guilty.

CONVINCE *v.*
To persuade or satisfy the mind by evidence; to subdue the opposition of the mind to truth, or to what is alledged, and compel it to yield its assent.

CONVOCATION *n.*
1. The act of calling or assembling by summons.
2. An assembly.

CORNET *n.*
An instrument of music, in the nature of a trumpet, sounded by blowing with the mouth. It was of a winding shape like a horn.

CORRUPT *v.*
1. To change from a sound to a putrid or putrescent state.
2. To vitiate or deprave; to change from good to bad.
3. To waste, spoil or consume.
4. To defile or pollute.
5. To entice from good and allure to evil.
6. To pervert; to break, disobey or make void.

CORRUPT *a.*
1. Changed from a sound to a putrid state.
2. Spoiled; tainted; vitiated; unsound.
3. Depraved; vitiated; tainted with wickedness.
4. Debased; rendered impure; changed to a worse state.
5. Not genuine; infected with errors or mistakes.

COTE *n.*
A shed or inclosure for beasts.

COUCH *v.*
1. To lay down; to repose on a bed or place of rest.
2. To stoop; to bend the body or back; to lower in reverence, or to bend under

labor, pain, or a burden.

COUCH *n.*
A bed; a place for rest or sleep.

COULTER *n.*
The fore iron of a plow, with a sharp edge, that cuts the earth or sod.

COUNTENANCE *n.*
The contents of a body; the outline and extent which constitutes the whole figure or external appearance.

COUNTENANCE *v.*
1. To favor; to encourage by opinion or words.
2. To aid; to support; to encourage; to abet; to vindicate.

COUNTERVAIL *v.*
To act against with equal force, or power; to equal; to act with equivalent effect against any thing; to balance; to compensate.

COUNTERVAIL *n.*
Equal weight or strength; power or value sufficient to obviate any effect; equal weight or value; compensation; requital.

COURTEOUS *a.*
Polite; wellbred; being of elegant manners; civil; obliging; condescending.

COVENANT *n.*
A mutual consent or agreement of two or more persons, to do or to forbear some act or thing; a contract; stipulation.

COVENANT *v.*
To enter into a formal agreement; to stipulate; to bind ones self by contract.

COVERT *n.*
A covering, or covering place; a place which covers and shelters; a shelter; a defense.

COVET *v.*
To desire or wish for, with eagerness; to desire earnestly to obtain or possess.

CRACKNEL *n.*
A hard brittle cake or biscuit.

CRAG *n.*
A steep rugged rock; a rough broken rock, or point of a rock.

CREDITOR *n.*
A person to whom a sum of money or other thing is due, by obligation, promise or in law.

CRIB *n.*
The manger of a stable, in which oxen and cows feed.

CRISPING *v.*
Curling; frizzling.

CROP *n.*
The first stomach of a fowl; the craw.

CROP *v.*
To cut off the ends of any thing; to eat off; to pull off; to pluck; to mow; to reap.

CRUCIFY *v.*
1. To nail to a cross; to put to death by nailing the hands and feet to a cross or gibbet.
2. To subdue; to mortify; to destroy the power or ruling influence of.

CRUSE *n.*
A small cup.

CUBIT *n.*
The length of a mans arm from the elbow to the ex-tremity of the middle fin-ger.

CUMBER *v.*
To perplex or embarrass; to distract or trouble.

CUMBRANCE *n.*
That which obstructs, re-tards, or renders motion or action difficult and toil-some; burden; encum-brance; hindrance; oppres-sive load; embarrassment.

CUMMIN *n.*
An annual plant of one species, whose seeds have a bitterish warm taste, with an aromatic flavor.

CURDLE *v.*
To coagulate or concrete; to thicken, or change into curd.

CURIOUS *a.*
1. Wrought with care and art; elegant; neat; finished.
2. Requiring care and ni-cety.

CURSE *v.*
1. To utter a wish of evil against one; to imprecate evil upon; to call for mis-chief or injury to fall upon;

to execrate.

2. To injure; to subject to evil; to vex, harass or torment with great calamities.

3. To devote to evil.

4. To utter imprecations; to affirm or deny with imprecations of divine vengeance.

CURSE *n.*

1. Malediction; the expression of a wish of evil to another.

2. Imprecation of evil.

3. Affliction; torment; great vexation.

4. Condemnation; sentence of divine vengeance on sinners.

5. Denunciation of evil.

CURSED *v.*

1. Execrated; afflicted; vexed; tormented.

2. Devoted to destruction.

3. Deserving a curse; execrable; hateful; detestable; abominable.

DAGGER *n.*

A short sword; a poniard.

DAINTY *n.*

Something nice and delicate to the taste; that which is exquisitely delicious; a delicacy.

DAM *n.*

A female parent.

DAMN *v.*

1. To sentence to eternal torments in a future state; to punish in hell.

2. To condemn; to decide to be wrong or worthy of punishment; to censure; to reprobate.

DAMNABLE *a.*

That may be damned or condemned; deserving damnation; worthy of eternal punishment.

DAMNATION *n.*

1. Condemnation.

2. Sentence or condemnation to everlasting punishment.

DAMSEL *n.*

A young woman.

DANDLED *v.*

Danced on the knee, or in the arms; fondled; amused by trifles or play.

DARLING *a.*

Dearly beloved; favorite; regarded with great kindness and tenderness.

DASH *v.*
To strike and bruise or break; to break by collision.

DAUBED *v.*
Smeared with soft adhesive matter.

DAWNING *v.*
Growing light; first appearing luminous; opening.

DAYSMAN *n.*
An umpire or arbiter; a mediator.

DAYSPRING *n.*
The dawn; the beginning of the day, or first appearance of light.

DEACON *n.*
A minister or servant.

DEARTH *n.*
1. Scarcity.
2. Want; need; famine.
3. Barrenness; sterility.

DEBASE *v.*
To reduce from a higher to a lower state or grade of worth, dignity, purity, station, etc.; to degrade; to lower; to deteriorate; to abase.

DEBTOR *n.*
1. The person who owes another either money, goods or services.
2. One who is under obligation to do something.

DECEASE *n.*
Literally, departure; hence, departure from this life; death.

DECEIT *n.*
1. A catching or ensnaring.
2. The misleading of a person; the leading of another person to believe what is false, or not to believe what is true, and thus to ensnare him; fraud; fallacy; cheat; any declaration, artifice or practice, which misleads another, or causes him to believe what is false.
3. Stratagem; artifice; device intended to mislead.
4. That which is obtained by guile, fraud or oppression.

DECEIVE *v.*
1. To mislead the mind; to cause to err; to cause to

believe what is false, or disbelieve what is true; to impose on; to delude.
2. To beguile; to cheat.

DECLINE *v.*
To turn or bend aside; to deviate; to stray; to withdraw.

DECREE *n.*
1. Judicial decision, or determination of a litigated cause.
2. An order, edict or law made by a superior as a rule to govern inferiors.
3. Established law, or rule.

DECREE *v.*
1. To determine judicially; to resolve by sentence.
2. To determine or resolve legislatively; to fix or appoint; to set or constitute by edict or in purpose.

DEFAME *v.*
1. To slander; falsely and maliciously to utter words respecting another which tend to injure his reputation or occupation.
2. To speak evil of; to dishonor by false reports; to calumniate; to libel; to impair reputation by acts or words.

DEFER *v.*
To delay; to put off; to postpone to a future time.

DEFILE *v.*
1. To make unclean; to render foul or dirty.
2. To soil or sully; to tarnish.
3. To corrupt chastity; to debauch; to violate; to tarnish the purity of character by lewdness.
4. To taint; to corrupt; to vitiate; to render impure with sin.

DEFRAUD *v.*
1. To deprive of right, either by obtaining something by deception or artifice, or by taking something wrongfully without the knowledge or consent of the owner; to cheat; to cozen.
2. To withhold wrongfully from another what is due to him.
3. To prevent one wrongfully from obtaining what he may justly claim.

DEFY *v.*
1. To dare; to provoke to

combat or strife, by appealing to the courage of another; to invite one to contest; to challenge.

2. To dare; to brave; to offer to hazard a conflict by manifesting a contempt of opposition, attack or hostile force.

3. To challenge to say or do any thing.

DEGENERATE *v.*

To become worse; to decay in good qualities; to pass from a good to a bad or worse state; to lose or suffer a diminution of valuable qualities, either in the natural or moral world.

DEGENERATE *a.*

1. Having fallen from a perfect or good state into a less excellent or worse state; having lost something of the good qualities possessed; having declined in natural or moral worth.

2. Low; base; mean; corrupt; fallen from primitive or natural excellence; having lost the good qualities of the species.

DELECTABLE *a.*

Delightful; highly pleasing; that gives great joy or pleasure.

DELICACY *n.*

That which delights or pleases.

DELICATES *n.*

Anything nice; a nicety.

DELUSION *n.*

1. The act of deluding; deception; a misleading of the mind.

2. False representation; illusion; error or mistake proceeding from false views.

DEMAND *v.*

To ask; to question; to inquire.

DENOUNCE *v.*

1. To declare solemnly; to proclaim in a threatening manner; to announce or declare.

2. To threaten by some outward sign, or expression.

3. To inform against; to accuse.

DEPUTE *v.*

To appoint as a substitute or agent to act for another;

to appoint and send with a special commission or authority to transact business in anothers name.

DERIDE *v.*
To laugh at in contempt; to turn to ridicule or make sport of; to mock; to treat with scorn by laughter.

DERISION *n.*
1. The act of laughing at in contempt.
2. Contempt manifested by laughter; scorn.
3. An object of derision or contempt; a laughing-stock.

DESCRY *v.*
To espy; to explore; to examine by observation.

DESPAIR *n.*
Hopelessness; a hopeless state; a destitution of hope or expectation.

DESPAIR *v.*
To be without hope; to give up all hope or expectation.

DESPITE *n.*
1. Extreme malice; violent hatred; malignity; malice

irritated or enraged; active malignity; angry hatred.
2. Defiance with contempt, or contempt of opposition.

DESTITUTE *a.*
1. Not having or possessing; wanting.
2. Needy; abject; comfortless; friendless.

DETAIN *v.*
1. To keep back or from; to withhold.
2. To restrain from proceeding; to stay or stop; to delay.
3. To hold or keep in custody.

DETEST *v.*
To thrust away. To abhor; to abominate; to hate extremely.

DEVIL *n.*
1. An evil spirit or being; a fallen angel, expelled from heaven for rebellion against God; the chief of the apostate angels; the implacable enemy and tempter of the human race.
2. A very wicked person, and in ludicrous language, an great evil.
3. An idol, or false god.

DEVISE *v.*
1. To invent; to contrive;
to form in the mind by new
combinations of ideas, new
applications of principles,
or new arrangement of
parts; to excogitate; to
strike out by thought; to
plan; to scheme; to project.
2. To consider; to contrive;
to lay a plan; to form a
scheme.

DEVOUR *v.*
1. To eat up; to eat with
greediness; to eat raven-
ously.
2. To destroy; to consume
with rapidity and violence.
3. To annihilate; to con-
sume.
4. To waste; to spend in
dissipation and riot.
5. To destroy spiritually; to
ruin the soul.

DEVOUT *a.*
1. Yielding a solemn and
reverential attention to
God in religious exercises.
2. Pious; devoted to religion; religious.
3. Expressing devotion or
piety.
4. Sincere; solemn; ear-
nest.

DIADEM *n.*
1. Anciently, a head-band
or fillet worn by kings as a
badge or royalty.
2. A distinguished or principal ornament.

DIGNITY *n.*
1. True honor; nobleness
or elevation of mind, consisting in a high sense of
propriety, truth and justice,
with an abhorrence of
mean and sinful actions;
opposed to meanness.
2. Elevation; honorable
place or rank of elevation;
degree of excellence.

DILIGENCE *n.*
1. Steady application in
business of any kind; constant effort to accomplish
what is undertaken; exer-
tion of body or mind without unnecessary delay or
sloth; due attention; indus-
try; assiduity.
2. Care; heed; heedfulness.

DILIGENT *a.*
1. Steady in application to
business; constant in effort
or exertion to accomplish
what is undertaken; assiduous; attentive; industrious;
not idle or negligent.

2. Steadily applied; prosecuted with care and constant effort; careful; assiduous.

DIMINISH *v.*
To lessen; to make less or smaller, by any means; to degrade.

DISALLOW *v.*
1. To refuse permission, or not to permit; not to grant; not to make or suppose lawful; not to authorize; to disapprove.
2. To testify dislike or disapprobation; to refuse assent.
3. Not to approve; not to receive; to reject.
4. Not to allow or admit as just; to reject.

DISANNUL *v.*
To annul; to make void; to deprive of authority or force; to nullify; to abolish.

DISCERN *v.*
1. To separate by the eye, or by the understanding.
2. To distinguish; to see the difference between two or more things; to discriminate.
3. To make the difference.

4. To discover; to see; to distinguish by the eye.
5. To discover by the intellect; to distinguish; to have knowledge of; to judge.

DISCHARGE *n.*
1. Release from obligation, debt or penalty.
2. Exemption; escape.

DISCIPLE *n.*
1. A learner; a scholar; one who receives or professes to receive instruction from another.
2. A follower; an adherent to the doctrines of another.

DISCIPLE *v.*
1. To teach; to train, or bring up.
2. To make disciples of; to convert to doctrines or principles.

DISCIPLINE *n.*
1. Education; instruction; cultivation and improvement.
2. Instruction and government, comprehending the communication of knowledge and the regulation of practice.
3. Rule of government; method of regulating prin-

ciples and practice.

4. Subjection to laws, rules, order, precepts or regulations.

5. Correction; chastisement; punishment intended to correct crimes or errors.

DISCIPLINE *v.*

1. To instruct or educate; to inform the mind; to prepare by instructing in correct principles and habits.

2. To instruct and govern; to teach rules and practice, and accustom to order and subordination.

3. To correct; to chastise; to punish.

4. To advance and prepare by instruction.

DISCOMFIT *v.*

To rout; to defeat; to scatter in fight; to cause to flee; to vanquish.

DISCOMFITURE *n.*

Rout; defeat in battle; dispersion; overthrow.

DISCONTENT *n.*

Want of content; uneasiness or inquietude of mind; dissatisfaction at any present state of things.

DISCORD *n.*

1. Disagreement among persons or things.

2. Disagreement; want of order; a clashing.

DISCREET *a.*

Prudent; wise in avoiding errors or evil, and in selecting the best means to accomplish a purpose; circumspect; cautious; wary; not rash.

DISCRETION *n.*

1. Prudence, or knowledge and prudence; that discernment which enables a person to judge critically of what is correct and proper, united with caution; nice discernment and judgment, directed by circumspection.

2. Liberty or power of acting without other control than ones own judgment.

DISDAIN *v.*

To think unworthy; to deem worthless; to consider to be unworthy of notice, care, regard, esteem, or unworthy of ones character; to scorn; to contemn.

DISMAY *v.*
To deprive of that strength or firmness of mind which constitutes courage; to discourage; to dishearten; to sink or depress the spirits or resolution.

DISMAY *n.*
Fall or loss of courage; a sinking of the spirits; depression; dejection; a yielding to fear; that loss of firmness which is effected by fear or terror; fear impressed.

DISOBEDIENT *a.*
1. Neglecting or refusing to obey; omitting to do what is commanded, or doing what is prohibited; refractory; not observant of duty or rules prescribed by authority.
2. Not yielding to exciting force or power.

DISPATCH *v.*
1. To perform; to execute speedily; to finish.
2. To send out of the world; to put to death.

DISPENSATION *n.*
1. Distribution; the act of dealing out to different persons or places.
2. The dealing of God to his creatures; the distribution of good and evil, natural or moral, in the divine government.
3. That which is dispensed or bestowed; a system of principles and rites enjoined.

DISPERSE *v.*
1. To scatter; to drive asunder; to cause to separate into different parts.
2. To diffuse; to spread.
3. To dissipate.
4. To distribute.

DISPOSE *v.*
1. To regulate; to adjust; to set in right order.
2. To direct the course of a thing.

DISPOSITION *n.*
Manner in which things or the parts of a complex body are placed or arranged; order; method; distribution; arrangement.

DISPUTATION *n.*
The act of disputing; a reasoning or argumentation in opposition to something, or on opposite sides; contro-

versy in words; verbal contest, respecting the truth of some fact, opinion, proposition or argument.

DISPUTE *v.*

1. To contend in argument; to reason or argue in opposition; to debate; to altercate.
2. To strive or contend in opposition in a competitor.
3. To call in question the propriety of; to oppose by reasoning.

DISQUIET *v.*

To disturb; to deprive of peace, rest or tranquility; to make uneasy or restless; to harass the body; to fret or vex the mind.

DISSEMBLE *v.*

To be hypocritical; to assume a false appearance; to conceal the real fact, motives, intention or sentiments under some pretense.

DISSEMBLER *n.*

One who dissembles; a hypocrite; one who conceals his opinions or dispositions under a false appearance.

DISSENSION *n.*

Disagreement in opinion; contention in words; strife; discord; quarrel; breach of friendship and union.

DISSIMULATION *n.*

The act of dissembling; a hiding under a false appearance; a feigning; false pretension; hypocrisy.

DISTAFF *n.*

The staff of a spinning-wheel, to which a bunch of flax or tow is tied, and from which the thread is drawn.

DIVERS *a.*

Different; various.

DIVERSITY *n.*

Difference; dissimilitude; unlikeness; variety.

DIVINATION *n.*

1. The act of divining; a foretelling future events, or discovering things secret or obscure, by the aid of superior beings, or by other than human means.
2. Conjectural presage; prediction.

DIVINE *a.*

1. Pertaining to the true God.
2. Partaking of the nature of God.

DIVINE *v.*
1. To foreknow; to foretell; to presage.
2. To use or practice divination.
3. To utter presages or prognostications.

DOCTOR *n.*
1. A teacher.
2. A learned man; a man skilled in a profession; a man of erudition.

DOCTRINE *n.*
1. Whatever is taught.
2. The act of teaching.
3. Learning; knowledge.
4. The truths of the gospel in general.
5. Instruction and confirmation in the truths of the gospel.

DOLEFUL *a.*
1. Sorrowful; expressing grief.
2. Melancholy; sad; afflicted.
3. Dismal; impressing sorrow; gloomy.

DOMINION *n.*
1. Sovereign or supreme authority; the power of governing and controlling.
2. Power to direct, control, use and dispose of at pleasure; right of possession and use without being accountable.
3. An order of angels.
4. Persons governed.

DOTE *v.*
1. To be delirious; to have the intellect impaired by age, so that the mind wanders or wavers; to be silly.
2. To be excessively in love; usually with on or upon.

DOTH *present tense of do.*

DOUBT *v.*
1. A fluctuation of mind respecting truth or propriety, arising from defect of knowledge or evidence; uncertainty of mind; suspense; unsettled state of opinion.
2. Uncertainty of condition.
3. Suspicion; fear; apprehension.

DOWNSITTING *n.*

The act of sitting down; repose; a resting.

DOWRY *n.*
1. The money, goods or estate which a woman brings to her husband in marriage; the portion given with a wife.
2. The reward paid for a wife.

DRAG *n.*
Something to be drawn along the ground.

DRAGON *n.*
1. A large marine fish or serpent.
2. A venomous land serpent.
3. The devil.

DRAM *n.*
A weight of the eighth part of an ounce, or sixty grains.

DRAUGHT *n.*
1. The act of drawing a net; a sweeping for fish.
2. That which is taken by sweeping with a net.
3. A sink or drain.

DRAVE *participle of drive.*

DREAD *n.*
1. Great fear, or apprehension of evil or danger.
2. Awe; fear united with respect.
3. Terror.
4. The cause of fear; the person or the thing dreaded.

DREGS *n.*
1. That which is drained or thrown off, or that which subsides.
2. The sediment of liquors; lees; grounds; feculence; any foreign matter of liquors that subsides to the bottom of a vessel.
3. Waste or worthless matter; dross; sweepings; refuse.

DREW *past tense of draw.* (1913)

DROMEDARY *n.*
A species of camel, called also the Arabian camel, with one bunch or protuberance on the back.

DROPSY *n.*
An unnatural collection of water, in an part of the body, proceeding from a greater effusion of serum

by the exhalant arteries, than the absorbents take up.

DROSS *n.*
Waste matter; refuse; any worthless matter separated from the better part; impure matter.

DROUGHT *n.*
Dryness; want of rain or of water.

DROVE *past tense of drive.*

DROVE *n.*
A collection of cattle driven; a number of animals, as oxen, sheep or swine, driven in a body.

DRUNKARD *n.*
One given to ebriety or an excessive used of strong liquor; a person who habitually or frequently is drunk.

DRYSHOD *a.*
Without wetting the feet.

DUE *n.*
Owed; that ought to be paid or done to another.

DUKE *n.*
A chief; a prince.

DULCIMER *n.*
An instrument of music played by striking brass wires with little sticks.

DUMB *a.*
1. Mute; silent; not speaking.
2. Destitute of the power of speech; unable to utter articulate sounds; as the dumb brutes.

DUNG *n.*
The excrement of animals.

DUNGHILL *n.*
1. A heap of dung.
2. Any mean situation or condition.

DURETH *v.* (1913)
To last; to continue; to endure.

DURST *past tense of dare.*

EAR *n.*
1. A favorable hearing; attention; heed; regard.
2. The spike of corn.

EARING *n.*
A plowing of land.

EARNEST *a.*
1. Ardent in the pursuit of an object; eager to obtain; having a longing desire; warmly engaged or incited.
2. Ardent; warm; eager; zealous; animated; importunate.
3. Intent; fixed.

EARNEST *n.*
First fruits; that which is in advance, and gives promise of something to come.

EASE *n.*
1. Rest; an undisturbed state.
2. A quiet state; tranquillity; freedom from pain, concern, anxiety, solicitude, or any thing that frets or ruffles the mind.

EASTER *n.*
A festival of the Christian church observed in commemoration of our Savior's resurrection. It answers to the pascha or Passover of the Hebrews, and most nations still give it this name, pascha, pask, paque.

EBENEZER *n.* (Strongs)
Stone of the help.

EDIFY *v.*
1. To build.
2. To instruct and improve the mind in moral and religious knowledge, in faith and holiness.

EFFECTUAL *a.*
Producing an effect, or the effect desired or intended; having adequate power or force to produce the effect.

EFFEMINATE *a.*
1. Having the qualities of the female sex; soft or delicate to an unmanly degree; tender; womanish; voluptuous.
2. Womanish; weak; resembling the practice or qualities of the sex.

ELDER *n.*
1. One who is older than another or others.
2. A person advanced in life, and who, on account of his age, experience and wisdom, is selected for office.
3. An ancestor.

ELDEST *a.*
Oldest; most advanced in age; that was born before others; as the eldest son or

daughter.

ELECT *n.*
1. One chosen or set apart.
2. Chosen or designated by God to salvation.
3. Chosen; selected; set apart as a peculiar church and people.

ELECTION *n.*
1. The act of choosing a person to fill an office or employment, by any manifestation of preference.
2. Divine choice; predetermination of God.
3. Those who are elected.

ELOQUENT *a.*
Composed with elegance and spirit; elegant and animated; adapted to please, affect and persuade.

EMBALM *v.*
To open a dead body, take out the intestines, and fill their place with odoriferous and desiccative spices and drugs, to prevent its putrefaction.

EMBOLDEN *v.*
To give boldness or courage; to encourage.

EMBRACE *v.*
1. To take, clasp or inclose in the arms; to press to the bosom, in token of affection.
2. To comprehend; to include or take in.
3. To receive; to admit.

EMBROIDER *v.*
To border with ornamental needle-work, or figures; to adorn with raised figures of needle-work.

EMINENT *a.*
High; lofty.

EMRODS *n.*
Hemorrhoids; piles; a dilatation of the veins about the rectum, with a discharge of blood.

EMULATION *n.*
1. An ardor kindled by the praise-worthy examples of others, inciting to imitate them, or to equal or excel them.
2. Contest; contention; strife; competition; rivalry accompanied with a desire of depressing another.

ENCAMP *v.*
To pitch tents or form huts;

to halt on a march, spread tents and remain for a night or for a longer time.

ENCHANTER *n.*

One who enchants; a sorcerer or magician; one who has spirits or demons at his command; one who practices enchantment, or pretends to perform surprising things by the agency of demons.

ENCHANTMENT *n.*

The act of producing certain wonderful effects by the invocation or aid of demons, or the agency of certain supposed spirits; the use of magic arts, spells or charms; incantation.

ENCOURAGE *v.*

To give courage to; to give or increase confidence of success; to inspire with courage, spirit, or strength of mind; to embolden; to animate; to incite; to inspirit.

ENDANGER *v.*

To put in hazard; to bring into danger or peril; to expose to loss or injury.

ENDEAVOR *n.*

An effort; an essay; an attempt; an exertion of physical strength, or the intellectual powers, towards the attainment of an object.

ENDEAVOUR *v.*

To exert physical strength or intellectual power, for the accomplishment of an object; to try; to essay; to attempt.

ENDOW *v.*

1. To furnish with a portion of goods or estate, called dower.
2. To enrich or furnish with any gift, quality or faculty; to indue.

ENDURE *v.*

1. To last; to continue in the same state without perishing; to remain; to abide.
2. To bear; to brook; to suffer without resistance, or without yielding.
3. To bear with patience; to bear without opposition or sinking under the pressure.

ENGAGE *v.*

To embark in an affair.

ENGINE *n.*
A military machine.

ENGRAFT *v.*
To ingraft, which see.

ENGRAVE *v.*
1. To cut, as metals, stones or other hard substances, with a chisel or graver; to cut figures, letters or devices, on stone or metal; to mark by incision.
2. To imprint; to impress deeply; to infix.

ENJOIN *v.*
To order or direct with urgency; to admonish or instruct with authority; to command.

ENLARGE *v.*
To make greater in quantity or dimensions; to extend in limits, breadth or side; to expand in bulk.

ENLIGHTEN *v.*
1. To make light; to shed light on; to supply with light; to illuminate.
2. To quicken in the faculty of vision; to enable to see more clearly.
3. To give light to; to give clearer views; to illuminate; to instruct; to enable to see or comprehend truth.
4. To illuminate with divine knowledge, or a knowledge of the truth.

ENMITY *n.*
The quality of being an enemy; the opposite of friendship; ill will; hatred; unfriendly dispositions; malevolence.

ENQUIRE *v.*
1. To ask a question; to seek for truth or information by asking questions.
2. To seek for truth by argument or the discussion of questions, or by investigation.

ENRICH *v.*
To make rich, wealthy or opulent; to supply with abundant property.

ENSAMPLE *n.*
An example; a pattern or model for imitation.

ENSIGN *n.*
1. The flag or banner of a military band; a banner of colors; a standard; a figured cloth or piece of silk, attached to a staff.

2. Any signal to assemble or to give notice.

ENSNARE *v.*
To inveigle; to seduce by artifice; to take by wiles, stratagem or deceit.

ENSUE *v.*
To follow; to pursue.

ENTANGLE *v.*
1. To twist or interweave in such a manner as not to be easily separated; to make confused or disordered.
2. To insnare by captious questions; to catch; to perplex; to involve in contradictions.
3. To perplex or distract.

ENTERPRISE *n.*
That which is undertaken, or attempted to be performed; an attempt; a project attempted.

ENTERTAIN *v.*
To receive into the house and treat with hospitality.

ENTICE *v.*
1. To incite or instigate, by exciting hope or desire.
2. To tempt; to incite; to

urge or lead astray.

ENTREAT *v.*
To make an earnest petition or request.

ENVIOUS *a.*
Feeling or harboring envy; repining or feeling uneasiness, at a view of the excellence, prosperity or happiness of another; pained by the desire of possessing some superior good which another possesses.

ENVIRON *v.*
To surround; to encompass; to encircle.

ENVY *v.*
1. To feel uneasiness, mortification or discontent, at the sight of superior excellence, reputation or happiness enjoyed by another; to repine at another's prosperity; to fret or grieve one's self at the real or supposed superiority of another.
2. To grudge; to withhold maliciously.

EPHAH *n.*
A Hebrew measure of three pecks and three pints, or according to others, of

seven gallons and four pints, or about 15 solid inches.

EPHOD *n.*
A part of the sacerdotal habit, being a kind of girdle, which was brought from behind the neck over the two shoulders, and hanging down before, was put across the stomach, then carried round the waist and used as a girdle to the tunic. On the part in front were two precious stones, on which were engraved the names of the twelve tribes of Israel.

EPISTLE *n.*
A writing, directed or sent, communicating intelligence to a distant person; a letter; a letter missive.

EQUITY *n.*
1. Justice; right.
2. Impartiality; a just regard to right or claim.

ERE *adv.*
Before; sooner than.

ERRAND *n.*
1. A verbal message; a mandate or order; something to be told or done; a communication to be made to some person at a distance.
2. Any special business to be transacted by a messenger.

ERR *v.*
1. To wander from the right way; to deviate from the true course or purpose.
2. To miss the right way, in morals or religion; to deviate from the path or line of duty; to stray by design or mistake.

ESCHEW *v.*
To flee from; to shun; to avoid.

ESPOUSE *v.*
To betroth; to promise or engage in marriage, by contract in writing, or by some pledge.

ESPY *v.*
1. To see at a distance; to have the first sight of a thing remove.
2. To see or discover something intended to be hid, or in a degree concealed and not very visible.
3. To discover unexpect-

edly.
4. To inspect narrowly; to examine and make discoveries.

ESTABLISH *v.*
1. To set and fix firmly or unalterably; to settle permanently.
2. To make firm; to confirm; to ratify what has been previously set or made.
3. To settle or fix what is wavering, doubtful or weak; to confirm.
4. To confirm; to fulfill; to make good.
5. To set up in the place of another and confirm.

ESTATE *n.*
1. In a general sense, fixedness; a fixed condition.
2. Condition or circumstances of any person or thing, whether high or low.
3. Orders or classes of men in society or government.

ESTEEM *v.*
1. To set a value on, whether high or low; to estimate; to value.
2. To prize; to set a high value on; to regard with reverence, respect or friendship.
3. To hold in opinion; to repute; to think.

ESTIMATE *v.*
To judge and form an opinion of the value of; to rate by judgment or opinion, without weighing or measuring either value, degree, extent or quantity.

ESTRANGED *v.*
Withdrawn; withheld; alienated.

ETERNAL *a.*
1. Without beginning or end of existence.
2. Without end of existence or duration; everlasting; endless; immortal.
3. Perpetual; ceaseless; continued without intermission.
4. Unchangeable; existing at all times without change.

ETERNITY *n.*
Duration or continuance without beginning or end.

EUNUCH *n.*
A male of the human species castrated.

EUROCLYDON *n.*
A tempestuous wind, which drove ashore, on Malta, the ship in which Paul was sailing to Italy.

EVANGELIST *n.*
1. A writer of the history, or doctrines, precepts, actions, life and death of our blessed Savior, Jesus Christ.
2. A preacher or publisher of the gospel of Jesus Christ.

EVEN *n.*
Evening.

EVENTIDE *n.* (1913)
The time of evening.

EVERMORE *adv.*
Always; at all times.

EVIDENCE *n.*
1. That which elucidates and enables the mind to see truth; proof arising from our own perceptions by the senses, or from the testimony of others, or from inductions of reason.
2. Any instrument or writing which contains proof.

EVIDENT *a.*

Plain; open to be seen; clear to the mental eye; apparent; manifest.

EVIL *a.*
1. Having bad qualities of a natural kind; mischievous; having qualities which tend to injury, or to produce mischief.
2. Having bad qualities of a moral kind; wicked; corrupt; perverse; wrong; evil deeds; evil speaking.
3. Unfortunate; unhappy; producing sorrow, distress, injury or calamity.

EVIL *n.*
1. Misfortune; mischief; injury.
2. Depravity; corruption of heart, or disposition to commit wickedness; malignity.
3. Malady.

EVIL *adv.*
1. Not well; not with justice or propriety; unsuitable.
2. Not virtuously; not innocently.
3. Not happily; unfortunately.
4. Injuriously; not kindly.

EWE *n.*
A female sheep; the female of the ovine race of animals.

EXACT *v.*
1. To force or compel to pay or yield; to demand or require authoritatively; to extort by means of authority or without pity or justice.
2. To demand or right.
3. To demand of necessity; to enforce a yielding or compliance; or to enjoin with pressing urgency.

EXACTOR *n.*
1. One who exacts; an officer who collects tribute, taxes or customs.
2. An extortioner; one who compels another to pay more than is legal or reasonable; one who demands something without pity or regard to justice.
3. He that demands by authority.
4. One who is unreasonably severe in his injunctions or demands.

EXALT *v.*
To raise high; to elevate.

EXAMINE *v.*
1. To inspect carefully, with a view to discover truth or the real state of a thing.
2. To try by a rule or law.

EXAMPLE *n.*
1. A pattern; a copy; a mode; that which is proposed to be imitated.
2. A pattern, in morals or manners; a copy, or model; that which is proposed or is proper to be imitated.
3. Precedent or former instance, in a bad sense, intended for caution.
4. A person fit to be proposed for a pattern; one whose conduct is worthy of imitation.
5. Instance serving for illustration of a rule or precept.

EXCEED *v.*
1. To pass or go beyond; to proceed beyond any given or supposed limit, measure or quantity, or beyond any thing else.
2. To surpass; to excel.

EXCEED *v.*
1. To go too far; to pass the proper bounds; to go

over any given limit, number or measure.
2. To bear the greater proportion; to be more or larger.

EXCEEDING *v.*
1. Going beyond; surpassing; excelling; outdoing.
2. Great in extent, quantity or duration; very extensive.

EXCEL *v.*
1. To go beyond; to exceed; to surpass in good qualities or laudable deeds; to outdo.
2. To exceed or go beyond in bad qualities or deeds.
3. To exceed; to surpass.

EXCELLENCY *n.*
1. The state of possessing good qualities in an unusual or eminent degree; the state of excelling in any thing.
2. Dignity; high rank in the scale of beings.

EXCESS *n.*
1. That which exceeds any measure or limit, or which exceeds something else, or a going beyond a just line or point.
2. Any transgression of due limits.
3. Any indulgence of appetite, passion or exertion, beyond the rules of God's word, or beyond any rule of propriety; intemperance in gratifications.

EXCLUDE *v.*
To thrust out or eject.

EXECRATION *n.*
The act of cursing; a curse pronounced; imprecation of evil; utter detestation expressed.

EXECUTE *v.*
1. To perform; to do; to effect; to carry into complete effect; to complete; to finish.
2. To inflict.
3. To carry into effect the law, or the judgment or sentence on a person.

EXECUTIONER *n.*
One who executes; one who carries into effect a judgment of death; one who inflicts a capital punishment.

EXEMPT *v.*
To take out or from; to free, or permit to be free,

from any charge, burden, restraint, duty, evil or requisition, to which others are subject; to privilege; to grant immunity from.

EXEMPT *a.*
Free; clear; not included.

EXERCISE *n.*
1. Any kind of work, labor or exertion of body.
2. Use; practice; the exertions and movements customary in the performance of business.
3. Practice; performance.
4. Use; employment; exertion.

EXHORT *v.*
1. To incite by words or advice; to animate or urge by arguments to a good deed or to any laudable conduct or course of action.
2. To advise; to warn; to caution.
3. To incite or stimulate to exertion.
4. To deliver exhortation; to use words or arguments to incite to good deeds.

EXILE *n.*
The person banished, or

expelled from his country by authority.

EXORCIST *n.*
One who pretends to expel evil spirits by conjuration, prayers, and ceremonies.

EXPEDIENT *a.*
1. Hastening; urging forward.
2. Tending to promote the object proposed; fit or suitable for the purpose; proper under the circumstances.
3. Useful; profitable.
4. Quick; expeditious.

EXPEL *v.*
1. To drive out; to force to leave.
2. To eject; to throw out.
3. To banish; to exile.

EXPIRE *v.*
1. To perish; to end; to fail or be destroyed; to come to nothing; to be frustrated.
2. To come to an end; to cease; to terminate; to close or conclude.

EXPLOIT *n.*
A deed or act; more especially, a heroic act; a deed of renown; a great or noble

achievement.

EXPOUND *v.*
To explain; to lay open the meaning; to clear of obscurity; to interpret.

EXPRESS *v.*
1. To utter; to declare in words; to speak.
2. To press or squeeze out; to force out by pressure.

EXPRESS *a.*
1. Plain; clear; expressed.
2. Given in direct terms; not implied or left to inference.
3. Copied; resembling; bearing an exact representation.

EXPRESSLY *adv.*
In direct terms; plainly.

EXTINCT *a.*
1. Extinguished; put out; quenched.
2. Being at an end; having no survivor.
3. Being at an end; having ceased.
4. Being at an end, by abolition or disuse; having no force.

EXTOL *v.*

To raise in words or eulogy; to praise; to exalt in commendation; to magnify.

EXTORTION *n.*
The act of extorting; the act or practice of wresting any thing from a person by force, duress, menaces, authority, or by any undue exercise of power; illegal exaction; illegal compulsion to pay money, or to do some other act.

EXTREMITY *n.*
1. The utmost point; the highest or furthest degree.
2. The utmost rigor or violence.

EYESALVE *n.*
Ointment for the eye.

EYESERVICE *n.*
Service performed only under inspection, or the eye of an employer.

EYEWITNESS *n.*
One who sees a thing done; one who has ocular view anything.

FABLE *n.*
1. A feigned story or tale,

intended to instruct or amuse.

2. Fiction in general.

3. An idle story; vicious or vulgar fictions.

FAIN *adv.*
Gladly; with joy or pleasure.

FAINT *a.*
1. Weak; feeble; languid; exhausted.

2. Imperfect; feeble; not striking.

3. Cowardly; timorous.

4. Dejected; depressed; dispirited.

FAIR *a.*
1. Clear; free from spots.

2. Beautiful; handsome; properly, having a handsome face.

3. Pleasing to the eye; handsome or beautiful in general.

4. Clear; not cloudy or overcast.

5. Free from stain or blemish; unspotted; untarnished.

FAITH *n.*
1. Belief; the assent of the mind to the truth of a proposition advanced by another; belief, or probable evidence of any kind.

2. The assent of the mind to the truth of divine revelation, on the authority of God's testimony, accompanied with a cordial assent of the will or approbation of the heart; an entire confidence or trust in God's character and declarations, and in the character and doctrines of Christ, with an unreserved surrender of the will to his guidance, and dependence on his merits for salvation.

3. The object of belief; a doctrine or system of doctrines believed; a system of revealed truths received by Christians.

4. The promises of God, or his truth and faithfulness.

5. An open profession of gospel truth.

6. A persuasion or belief of the lawfulness of things indifferent.

7. Faithfulness; fidelity; a strict adherence to duty and fulfillment of promises.

FAITHFUL *a.*
1. Firm in adherence to the truth and to the duties of

religion.

2. Firmly adhering to duty; of true fidelity; loyal; true to allegiance.

3. Constant in the performance of duties or services; exact in attending to commands.

4. True; exact; in conformity to the letter and spirit.

5. True to the marriage covenant.

6. Conformable to truth.

7. Constant; not fickle.

8. True; worthy of belief.

FAMILIARS *n.*

1. A demon or evil spirit supposed to attend at a call.

2. An intimate; a close companion.

FAMINE *n.*

1. Scarcity of food; dearth; a general want of provisions sufficient for the inhabitants of a country or besieged place.

2. Want; destitution.

FAMISH *v.*

1. To starve; to kill or destroy with hunger.

2. To exhaust the strength of, by hunger or thirst; to distress with hunger.

3. To kill by deprivation or denial of any thing necessary for life.

FAN *n.*

1. An instrument for winnowing grain, by moving which the grain is thrown up and agitated, and the chaff is separated and blown away.

2. An instrument to raise the fire or flame.

FAN *v.*

To winnow; to separate chaff from grain and drive it away by a current of air.

FANNER *n.*

One who fans.

FARE *v.*

1. To be in any state, good or bad; to be attended with any circumstances or train of events, fortunate or unfortunate.

2. To proceed in a train of consequences, good or bad.

FARE *n.*

The price of passage or going; the sum paid or due, for conveying a person by land or water.

FAREWELL *n.*
A wish of happiness or welfare at parting; the parting compliment; adieu.

FARTHING *n.*
1. The fourth of a penny.
2. Very small price or value. It is not worth a farthing, that is, it is of very little worth, or worth nothing.

FASHION *n.*
1. The make or form of any thing; the state of any thing with regard to its external appearance; shape.
2. Form; model to be imitated; pattern.

FASHION *v.*
1. To form; to give shape or figure to; to mold.
2. To fit; to adapt; to accommodate; with to.
3. To make according to the rule prescribed by custom.

FAST *v.*
1. To abstain from food, beyond the usual time; to omit to take the usual meals, for a time.
2. To abstain from food voluntarily, for the mortification of the body or appetites, or as a token of grief, sorrow and affliction.

FAST *n.*
1. Abstinence from food.
2. The time of fasting, whether a day, week or longer time.

FATHOM *n.*
A measure of length containing six feet, the space to which a man may extend his arms.

FATLING *n.*
A lamb, kid or other young animal fattened for slaughter; a fat animal.

FAULTY *a.*
Guilty of a fault or of faults; blamable; worthy of censure.

FEAR *n.*
1. A painful emotion or passion excited by an expectation of evil, or the apprehension of impending danger.
2. The cause of fear.
3. The object of fear.
4. A filial or a slavish passion.
5. The worship of God.

6. The law and word of God.
7. Reverence; respect; due regard.

FEAR *v.*
To be in apprehension of evil; to be afraid; to feel anxiety on account of some expected evil.

FEEBLE *a.*
1. Weak; destitute of much physical strength.
2. Debilitated by age or decline of life.
3. Not strong or vigorous.

FEEBLE-MINDED *a.*
Weak in mind; wanting firmness or constancy; ir-resolute.

FEET *plural of foot.*

FEIGN *v.*
1. To invent or imagine; to form an idea or conception of something not real.
2. To make a show of; to pretend; to assume a false appearance; to counterfeit.

FEIGNEDLY *adv.*
In fiction; in pretense; not really.

FELL *v.*
To cause to fall; to pros-trate; to bring to the ground, either by cutting, or by striking.

FELLER *n.*
One who hews or knocks down.

FELLOE *n.*
The exterior part or rim of a wheel, supported by the spokes.

FELLOW *n.*
1. A companion; an associ-ate.
2. One of the same kind.
3. An equal.

FELLOWSHIP *n.*
1. Companionship; soci-ety; consort; mutual asso-ciation of persons on equal and friendly terms; famil-iar intercourse.
2. Partnership; joint inter-est.
3. Company; a state of be-ing together.
4. Communion; intimate familiarity.

FEN *n.*
Low land overflowed, or covered wholly or partially

with water, but producing sedge, coarse grasses, or other aquatic plants; boggy land; a moor or marsh.

FENCED *v.*
Inclosed with a fence; guarded; fortified.

FERRET *n.*
An animal of the genus Mustela, or Weasel kind, about 14 inches in length, of a pale yellow color with red eyes.

FERVENT *a.*
1. Hot; boiling.
2. Hot in temper; vehement.
3. Ardent; very warm; earnest; excited; animated; glowing.

FETTER *n.*
1. A chain for the feet; a chain by which an animal is confined by the foot, either made fast or fixed, as a prisoner, or impeded in motion and hindered from leaping.
2. Any thing that confines or restrains from motion.

FIDELITY *n.*
1. Faithfulness; careful and exact observance of duty, or performance of obligations.
2. Honesty; veracity; adherence to truth.

FILLET *n.*
A little band.

FINING *v.*
1. Clarifying; refining; purifying; defecating; separating from extraneous matter.
2. Imposing a fine or pecuniary penalty.

FIREBRAND *n.*
A piece of wood kindled or on fire.

FIRKIN *n.*
A measure of capacity, being the fourth part of a barrel.

FIRMAMENT *n.*
The region of the air; the sky or heavens.

FIRSTLING *n.*
The first produce or offspring.

FITCH *n.*
A chick-pea.

FITLY *adv.*
1. Suitably; properly; with propriety.
2. Commodiously; conveniently.

FLAG *n.*
A flat stone, or a pavement of flat stones.

FLAGON *n.*
A vessel with a narrow mouth, used for holding and conveying liquors.

FLANK *n.*
The fleshy or muscular part of the side of an animal, between the ribs and the hip.

FLATTER *v.*
1. To soothe by praise; to gratify self-love by praise or obsequiousness; to please a person by applause or favorable notice, by respectful attention, or by any thing that exalts him in his own estimation, or confirms his good opinion of himself.
2. To please; to gratify.
3. To praise falsely; to encourage by favorable notice.
4. To raise false hopes by representations not well founded.

FLAX *n.*
A plant of the genus Linum, consisting of a single slender stalk, the skin or herl of which is used for making thread and cloth, called linen, cambric, lawn, lace, &c.

FLAY *v.*
1. To skin; to strip off the skin of an animal.
2. To take off the skin or surface of any thing.

FLED *past tense of flee.*

FLEE *v.*
1. To run with rapidity, as from danger; to attempt to escape; to hasten from danger or expected evil.
2. To depart; to leave; to hasten away.
3. To avoid; to keep at a distance from.

FLEECE *n.*
The coat of wool shorn from a sheep at one time.

FLEECE *v.*
1. To shear off a covering or growth of wool.

2. To strip of money or property; to take from, by severe exactions, under color of law or justice, or pretext of necessity, or by virtue of authority.
3. To spread over as with wool; to make white.

FLESH *n.*
1. The body.
2. Men in general; mankind.
3. The corruptible body of man.
4. Carnality; corporeal appetites.
5. The present life; the state of existence in this world.
6. Kindred; stock; family.

FLESHHOOK *n.*
A hook to draw flesh from a pot or caldron.

FLESHLY *a.*
1. Pertaining to the flesh; corporeal.
2. Carnal; worldly; lascivious.
3. Animal.
4. Human; not celestial; not spiritual or divine.

FLESHY *a.*
1. Full of flesh; plump; musculous.
2. Fat; gross; corpulent.
3. Corporeal.

FLOURISH *v.*
1. To thrive; to grow luxuriantly; to increase and enlarge.
2. To be prosperous; to increase in wealth or honor.
3. To grow in grace and in good works; to abound in the consolations of religion.

FLOWERS *n.*
The bloom or blossom of a plant; the showy portion.

FLUTTER *v.*
To move or flap the wings rapidly, without flying, or with short flights; to hover.

FLUX *n.*
Any flow or issue of matter.

FLUX *v.*
1. To melt; to fuse; to make fluid.
2. To salivate.

FODDER *n.*
Food or dry food for cattle, horses and sheep.

FOE *n.*
1. An enemy; one who entertains personal enmity, hatred, grudge or malice against another.
2. An enemy in war.
3. An opponent; an enemy; one who opposes any thing in principle; an ill-wisher.

FOLD *n.*
1. A pen or inclosure for sheep; a place where a flock of sheep is kept.
2. A flock of sheep; the church, the flock of the Shepherd of Israel.

FOLK *n.*
1. People in general, or any part of them without distinction.
2. Certain people, discriminated from others.

FOOL *n.*
1. One who is destitute of reason, or the common powers of understanding; an idiot.
2. A wicked or depraved person; one who acts contrary to sound wisdom in his moral deportment; one who follows his own inclinations, who prefers trifling and temporary pleas-ures to the service of God and eternal happiness.

FOOLISH *a.*
1. Void of understanding or sound judgment; weak in intellect.
2. Unwise; imprudent; acting without judgment or discretion in particular things.
3. Proceeding from folly, or marked with folly; silly; vain; trifling.
4. Wicked; sinful; acting without regard to the divine law and glory, or to one's own eternal happiness.
5. Proceeding from depravity; sinful.

FOOTMAN *n.*
A soldier who marches and fights on foot.

FORBAD *past tense of forbid.*

FORBARE *variant of forbear.*

FORBEAR *v.*
1. To stop; to cease; to hold from proceeding.
2. To pause; to delay.
3. To refuse; to decline.

4. To be patient; to restrain from action or violence.
5. To spare; to treat with indulgence and patience.
6. To withhold.

FORBEARANCE *n.*
1. The act of avoiding, shunning or omitting.
2. Command of temper; restraint of passions.
3. The exercise of patience; long suffering; indulgence towards those who injure us; lenity; delay of resentment or punishment.

FORBID *v.*
1. To prohibit; to interdict; to command to forbear or not to do.
2. To command not to enter.
3. To oppose; to hinder; to obstruct.
4. To utter a prohibition.

FORBORN *v. of forbear.*

FORCIBLE *a.*
1. Powerful; strong; mighty.
2. Violent; impetuous; driving forward with force.
3. Efficacious; active; powerful.

FORD *n.*
A place in a river or other water, where it may be passed by man or beast on foot, or by wading.

FOREFATHER *n.*
An ancestor; one who precedes another in the line of genealogy, in any degree.

FOREIGNER *n.*
A person born in a foreign country, or without the country or jurisdiction of which one speaks.

FOREKNOW *v.*
To have previous knowledge of; to foresee.

FOREKNOWLEDGE *n.*
Knowledge of a thing before it happens; prescience.

FOREORDAIN *v.*
To ordain or appoint before; to preordain; to predestinate; to predetermine.

FOREPART *n.*
1. The part first in time.
2. The part most advanced in place; the anterior part.
3. The beginning.

FORERUNNER *n.*

A messenger sent before to give notice of the approach of others; a harbinger.

FORESEE *v.*
To see beforehand; to see or know an event before it happens; to have pre-science of; to foreknow.

FORESCORE *a.*
Four times twenty; eighty.

FORETELL *v.*
1. To predict; to tell before an event happens; to prophesy.
2. To foretoken; to fore-show.

FOREWARN *v.*
1. To admonish before-hand.
2. To inform previously; to give previous notice.

FORFEIT *v.*
To lose or render confis-cable, by some fault, of-fense or crime; to lose the right to some species of property or that which be-longs to one; to alienate the right to possess by some neglect or crime.

FORGE *v.*

To make falsely; to falsify; to counterfeit; to make in the likeness of something else.

FORGIVE *v.*
1. To pardon; to remit; to overlook an offense, and treat the offender as not guilty.
2. To remit as a debt, fine or penalty.

FORNICATION *n.*
1. The incontinence or lewdness of unmarried per-sons, male or female; the criminal conversation of a married man with an un-married woman.
2. Adultery.
3. Incest.
4. Idolatry; a forsaking of the true God, and worship-ping of idols.

FORNICATOR *n.*
1. An unmarried person, male or female, who has criminal conversation with the other sex.
2. A married man who has sexual commerce with an unmarried woman.
3. A lewd person.
4. An idolater.

FORSAKE *v.*
1. To quit or leave entirely; to desert; to abandon; to depart from.
2. To abandon; to renounce; to reject.
3. To leave; to withdraw from; to fail.

FORSWEAR *v.*
1. To reject or renounce upon oath.
2. To deny upon oath.
3. To swear falsely; to commit perjury.

FORTH *adv.*
Forward; onward in time; in advance.

FORTH *prep.*
Out of.

FORTHWITH *adv. forth and with.*

FORTIFY *v.*
1. To surround with a wall, ditch, palisades or other works, with a view to defend against the attacks of an enemy; to strengthen and secure by forts, batteries and other works of art.
2. To strengthen against any attack.
3. To confirm; to add

strength and firmness to.
4. To furnish with strength or means of resisting force, violence or assault.

FORTRESS *n.*
1. Any fortified place; a fort; a castle; a strong hold; a place of defense or security.
2. Defense; safety; security.

FORWARD *adv.*
Toward a part or place before or in front; onward; progressively; go forward; move forward.

FOUL *a.*
1. Covered with or containing extraneous matter which is injurious, noxious or offensive; filthy; dirty; not clean.
2. Impure; polluted; defiling.
3. Wicked; detestable; abominable.

FOUL *v.*
To make filthy; to defile; to daub; to dirty; to bemire; to soil.

FOWL *n.*
A flying or winged animal;

the generic name of certain animals that move through the air by the aid of wings.

FOWLER *n.*
A sportsman who pursues wild fowls, or takes or kills them for food.

FRAIL *a.*
1. Weak; infirm; liable to fail and decay; subject to casualties; easily destroyed; perishable; not firm or durable.
2. Weak in mind or resolution; liable to error deception.

FRANKINCENSE *n.*
A dry resinous substance in pieces or drops; used as a perfume.

FRANKLY *adv.*
1. Openly; freely; ingenuously; without reserve, constraint or disguise.
2. Liberally; freely; readily.

FRAUD *n.*
Deceit; deception; trick; artifice by which the right or interest of another is injured; a stratagem intended to obtain some undue advantage; an attempt to gain or the obtaining of an advantage over another by imposition or immoral means.

FRAY *v.*
To fright; to terrify.

FREEWILL *n.*
1. The power of directing our own actions without restraint by necessity or fate.
2. Voluntariness; spontaneousness.

FRET *v.*
1. To agitate; to disturb; to make rough; to cause to ripple.
2. To tease; to irritate; to vex; to make angry.
3. To corrode; to gnaw; to ear away.

FRONTIER *n.*
The marches; the border, confine, or extreme part of a country, bordering on another country; the part furthest advanced, or the part that fronts an enemy, or which an invading enemy meets in front, or which fronts another country.

FRONTLET *n.*
A frontal or browband; a
fillet or band worn on the
forehead.

FROWARD *a.*
Perverse, that is, turning
from, with aversion or re-
luctance; not willing to
yield or comply with what
is required; unyielding;
ungovernable; refractory;
disobedient; peevish.

FRUSTRATE *v.*
1. To break or interrupt; to
defeat; to disappoint; to
balk; to bring to nothing.
2. To make null; to nullify;
to render of no effect.

FULLER *n.*
One whose occupation is
to full cloth.

FURBISH *v.*
To rub or scour to brightness; to polish; to burnish;
to furbish arms.

FURLONG *n.*
A measure of length; the
eighth part of a mile; forty
rods, poles or perches.

FURROW *n.*
1. A trench in the earth
made by a plow.
2. A long narrow trench or
channel in wood or metal;
a groove.
3. A hollow made by wrinkles in the face.

FURROW *v.*
1. To cut a furrow; to
make furrows in; to plow.
2. To make long narrow
channels or grooves in.
3. To cut; to make channels in; to plow.
4. To make hollows in by
wrinkles.

FURY *n.*
1. A violent rushing; impetuous motion.
2. Rage; a storm of anger;
madness; turbulence.
3. Enthusiasm; heat of the
mind.

GAD *v.*
1. To walk about; to rove
or ramble idly or without
any fixed purpose.
2. To ramble in growth.

GAINSAY *v.*
To contradict; to oppose in
words; to deny or declare
not to be true what another
says; to controvert; to dispute.

GALL *n.*
1. The bile, a bitter, a yellowish green fluid, secreted in the glandular substance of the liver.
2. Any thing extremely bitter.
3. Rancor; malignity.
4. Anger; bitterness of mind.

GALLANT *a.*
1. Brave; high-spirited; courageous; heroic; magnanimous.
2. Fine; noble.

GALLERY *n.*
A covered part of a building.

GALLEY *n.*
A low flat-built vessel, with one deck, and navigated with sails and oars.

GALLOWS *n.*
An instrument of punishment whereon criminals are executed by hanging.

GAPE *v.*
1. To open the mouth wide, from sleepiness, drowsiness or dullness; to yawn.
2. To open the mouth with a desire to injure or devour.

GARLANDS *n.*
1. A wreath or chaplet made of branches, flowers, fethers and sometimes of precious stones, to be worn on the head like a crown.
2. A ornament of flowers, fruits and leaves intermixed.

GARNER *n.*
A granary; a building or place where grain is stored for preservation.

GARNISH *v.*
To adorn; to decorate with appendages; to set off.

GARRISON *n.*
1. A body of troops stationed in a fort or fortified town, to defend it against an enemy, or to keep the inhabitants in subjection.
2. A fort, castle or fortified town, furnished with troops to defend it.
3. The state of being placed in a fortification for its defense.

GAT *past tense of get.*

GAY *a.*
1. Merry; airy; jovial; sportive; frolicksome.
2. Fine; showy.

GAZE *v.*
To fix the eyes and look steadily and earnestly; to look with eagerness or curiosity.

GENDER *v.*
1. To beget.
2. To copulate; to breed.

GENEALOGY *n.*
1. An account or history of the descent of a person or family from an ancestor; enumeration of ancestors and their children in the natural order of succession.
2. Pedigree; lineage; regular descent of a person or family from a progenitor.

GENTILE *n.*
A pagan; a worshipper of false gods; any person not a Jew or a Christian; a heathen.

GENTILE *a.*
Pertaining to pagans or heathens.

GHOST *n.*
Spirit; the soul of man.

GIN *n.*
A trap; a snare.

GIRD *v.*
1. To bind by surrounding with any flexible substance.
2. To make fast by binding; to put on.

GIRDLE *n.*
1. A band or belt; something drawn round the waist of a person, and tied or buckled.
2. Inclosure; circumference.

GIRDLE *v.*
To inclose; to enrivon; to shut in.

GIRT *v.*
To gird; to surround.

GLAD *a.*
1. Pleased; affected with pleasure or moderate joy; moderately happy.
2. Cheerful; joyous.
3. Cheerful; wearing the appearance of joy.

GLEAN *v.*
To gather stalks or ears of

grain left by reapers.

GLEDE *n.*
A fowl of the rapacious kind, the kite, a species of Falco.

GLISTERING *n.*
Shining; sparkling with light.

GLOOMINESS *n.*
1. Want of light; obscurity; darkness; dismalness.
2. Want of cheerfulness; cloudiness of look; heaviness of mind; melancholy.

GLORIFY *v.*
1. To praise; to magnify and honor in worship; to ascribe honor to, in thought or words.
2. To make glorious; to exalt to glory, or to celestial happiness.
3. To praise; to honor; to extol.

GLORIOUS *a.*
1. Illustrious; of exalted excellence and splendor; resplendent in majesty and divine attributes.
2. Noble; excellent; renowned; celebrated; illustrious; very honorable.

GLORY *n.*
1. Brightness; luster; splendor.
2. Splendor; magnificence.
3. Praise ascribed in adoration; honor.
4. The divine presence.

GLORY *v.*
1. To exult with joy; to rejoice.
2. To boast; to be proud of.

GLUTTON *n.*
1. One who indulges to excess in eating.
2. One eager of any thing to excess.

GLUTTONOUS *a.*
1. Given to excessive eating; indulging the appetite for food to excess.
2. Consisting in excessive eating.

GNASH *v.*
To strike the teeth together.

GOAD *n.*
A pointed instrument used to stimulate a beast to move faster.

GOD *n.*
1. The Supreme Being;

Jehovah; the eternal and infinite spirit, the creator, and the sovereign of the universe.

2. A false god; a heathen deity; an idol.

3. A prince; a ruler; a magistrate or judge; an angel.

4. Any person or thing exalted too much in estimation, or deified and honored as the chief good.

GODDESS *n.*
A female deity; a heathen deity of the female sex.

GODHEAD *n.*
Godship; deity; divinity; divine nature or essence.

GODLINESS *n.*
Piety; a religious life; a careful observance of the laws of God and performance of religious duties, proceeding from love and reverence for the divine character and commands; Christian obedience.

GODLY *a.*
1. Living in obedience to God's commands, from a principle of love to him and reverence of his character and precepts; religious; righteous.

2. Pious; conformed to God's law.

GODWARD *a.*
Toward God.

GOODLY *adv.*
Excellently.

GOODLY *a.*
1. Being of a handsome form; beautiful; graceful.

2. Pleasant; agreeable; desirable.

GOODMAN *n.*
A husband; the master of a family.

GORE *n.*
1. Blood; thick or clotted blood; blood that after effusion becomes inspissated.

2. Dirt; mud.

GORE *v.*
1. To stab; to pierce; to penetrate with a pointed instrument.

2. To pierce with the point of a horn.

GORGEOUS *a.*
Showy; fine; splendid; glittering with gay colors.

GOSPEL *n.*
1. The history of the birth, life, actions, death, resurrection, ascension and doctrines of Jesus Christ; a revelation of the grace of God to fallen man through a mediator, including the character, actions, and doctrines of Christ, with the whole scheme of salvation, as revealed by Christ and his apostles.
2. God's word.
3. Divinity; theology.
4. Any general doctrine.

GOURD *n.*
A plant and its fruit, of the genus Cucurbita.

GRACE *n.*
1. Favor; good will; kindness; disposition to oblige another.
2. The free unmerited love and favor of God, the spring and source of all the benefits men receive from him.
3. Favorable influence of God; divine influence or the influence of the spirit, in renewing the heart and restraining from sin.
4. The application of Christ's righteousness to the sinner.
5. A state of reconciliation to God.
6. Virtuous or religious affection or disposition.
7. Spiritual instruction, improvement and edification.
8. Eternal life; final salvation.
9. Favor; mercy; pardon.

GRAFF *v.*
1. To propagate by insertion or inoculation.
2. To insert in a body to which it did not originally belong.
3. To join one thing to another so as to receive support from it.

GRAVED *v.*
Carved; engraved.

GRAVEL *n.*
Small stones or fragments of stone, or very small pebbles, larger than the particles of sand, but often intermixed with them.

GRAVEN *v.*
Carved.

GRAVITY *n.* (1913)
Sobriety of character or

demeanor.

GREAVES *n.*
Armor for the legs; a sort of boots.

GREEDY *a.*
1. Having a keen appetite for food or drink; ravenous; voracious; very hungry.
2. Having a keen desire of any thing; eager to obtain.

GREET *v.*
1. To address with expressions of kind wishes; to salute in kindness and respect.
2. To pay compliments at a distance; to send kind wishes to.
3. To meet and address with kindness; or to express kind wishes accompanied with an embrace.

GRIEF *n.*
1. The pain of mind produced by loss, misfortune, injury or evils of any kind; sorrow; regret.
2. The pain of mind occasioned by our own misconduct; sorrow or regret that we have done wrong; pain accompanying repentance.

3. Cause of sorrow; that which afflicts.

GRIEVE *v.*
1. To give pain of mind to; to afflict; to wound the feelings.
2. To afflict; to inflict pain on.
3. To make sorrowful; to excite regret in.
4. To offend; to displease; to provoke.

GRISLED *a.*
Gray; of a mixed color.

GROSS *a.*
1. Thick; large; opposed to fine.
2. Stupid; dull.

GROVE *n.*
1. A small wood or cluster of trees with a shaded avenue, or a wood impervious to the rays of the sun.
2. A wood of small extent.
3. Something resembling a wood or trees in a wood.

GRUDGE *v.*
To be discontented at another's enjoyments or advantages; to envy one the possession or happiness which we desire for our-

selves.

GUILE *n.*
Craft; cunning; artifice;
duplicity; deceit.

GUILT *n.*
Criminality; that state of a
moral agent which results
from his actual commis-
sion of a crime or offense,
knowing it to be a crime,
or violation of law.

GUILTY *a.*
1. Criminal; having knowingly committed a crime or
offense, or having violated
a law by an overt act or by
neglect, and by that act or
neglect, being liable to
punishment; not innocent.
2. Wicked; corrupt; sinful.

GUTTER *n.*
A channel for water; a hollow piece of timber, or a
pipe, for catching and conveying off the water which
drops from the eaves of a
building.

HABERGEON *n.*
A coat of mail or armor to
defend the neck and breast.

HABITABLE *a.*

That may be inhabited or
dwelt in; capable of sus-
taining human beings.

HABITATION *n.*
Place of abode; a settled
dwelling; a mansion; a
house or other place in
which man or any animal
dwells.

HAFT *n.*
A handle; that part of an
instrument or vessel which
is taken into the hand, and
by which it is held and
used.

HAFT *v.*
To set in a haft; to furnish
with a handle.

HAIL *n.*
A wish of health; a salutation.

HALE *v.*
To pull or draw with force;
to drag.

HALLOW *v.*
1. To make holy; to consecrate; to set apart for holy
or religious use.
2. To devote to holy or religious exercises; to treat
as sacred.

3. To reverence; to honor as sacred.

HALT *v.*
1. To stop in walking; to hold.
2. To limp; that is, to stop with lameness.
3. To fail; to falter.

HALT *a.*
Lame; that is, holding or stopping in walking.

HANDBREADTH *n.*
A space equal to the breadth of the hand; a palm.

HANDMAIDEN *n.*
A maid that waits at hand; a female servant or attendant.

HANDSTAVE *n.*
A javelin.

HAP *v.*
To happen; to befall; to come by chance.

HAPLY *adv.*
By accident; casually.

HARDHEARTED *a.*
Cruel; pitiless; merciless; unfeeling; inhuman; inexo-rable.

HARE *n.*
A quadruped of the genus Lepus, with long ears, a short tail, soft hair, and a divided upper lip.

HARLOT *n.*
1. A woman who prostitutes her body for hire; a prostitute; a common woman.
2. One who forsakes the true God and worships idols.

HARNESS *n.*
Armor; the whole accouterments or equipments of a knight or horseman; defensive armor.

HARNESS *v.*
1. To put on the furniture of a horse for draught.
2. To defend; to equip or furnish for defense.

HARROW *n.*
An instrument of agriculture, formed of pieces of timber sometimes crossing each other, and set with iron teeth.

HARROW *v.*

To draw a harrow over, for the purpose of breaking clods and leveling the surface, or for covering seed sown.

HART *n.*
A stag or male deer, an animal of the cervine genus.

HAST
The second person singular of have.

HASTY *a.*
1. Quick; speedy; opposed to slow.
2. Eager precipitate; rash; opposed to deliberate.
3. Irritable; easily excited to wrath; passionate.

HATE *v.*
1. To dislike greatly; to have a great aversion to.
2. To love less.

HATE *n.*
Great dislike or aversion; hatred.

HATH *a.* (Strongs)
To Hold.

HAUGHTY *a.*
1. Proud and disdainful; having a high opinion of one's self, with some contempt for others; lofty and arrogant; supercilious.
2. Proceeding from excessive pride, or pride mingled with contempt; manifesting pride and disdain.
3. Proud and imperious.

HAVOCK *n.*
Waste; devastation; wide and general destruction.

HEADLONG *adv.*
With the head foremost.

HEADY *a.*
Rash; hasty; precipitate; violent; disposed to rush forward in an enterprise without thought or deliberation; hurried on by will or passion; ungovernable.

HEAR *v.*
1. To perceive by the ear; to feel an impression of sound by the proper organs.
2. To give audience or allowance to speak.
3. To attend; to listen; to obey.
4. To attend favorably; to regard.
5. To attend to the facts,

evidence, and arguments in a cause between parties; to try in a court of law or equity.

6. To learn.

7. To approve and embrace.

HEARKEN *v.*

1. To listen; to lend the ear; to attend to what is uttered, with eagerness or curiosity.

2. To attend; to regard; to give heed to what is uttered; to observe or obey.

HEART *n.*

1. A muscular viscus, which is the primary organ of the blood's motion in an animal body, situated in the thorax.

2. The inner part of any thing; the middle part or interior.

3. The chief part; the vital part; the vigorous or efficacious part.

4. The seat of the affections and passions.

5. The seat of the understanding.

6. The seat of the will; hence, secret purposes, intentions or designs.

HEARTH *n.*

A pavement or floor of brick or stone in a chimney, on which a fire is made to warm a room, and from which there is a passage for the smoke to ascend.

HEARTILY *adv.*

1. From the heart; with all the heart; with sincerity; really.

2. With zeal; actively; vigorously.

3. Eagerly; freely; largely.

HEATH *n.*

A plant of the genus Erica, of many species.

HEATHEN *n.*

A pagan; a Gentile; one who worships idols, or is unacquainted with the true God.

HEAVE *v.*

To lift; to raise; to move upward.

HEAVEN *n.*

1. The region or expanse which surrounds the earth, and which appears above and around us, like an immense arch or vault, in

which are seen the sun,
moon and stars.

2. The part of space in
which the omnipresent Je-
hovah is supposed to af-
ford more sensible mani-
festations of his glory.

3. The sky or air; the region of the atmosphere; or
an elevated place.

4. The Supreme Power; the
Sovereign of heaven; god.

HEBREW *n.*
A descendant of Jacob,
who was a descendant of
Eber; an Israelite; a Jew.

HEBREW *a.*
Pertaining to the Hebrews.

HEDGE *n.*
A thicket of thorn-bushes
or other shrubs or small
trees.

HEDGE *v.*
1. To inclose with a hedge;
to fence with a thicket of
shrubs or small trees; to
separate by a hedge.

2. To obstruct with a
hedge, or to obstruct in any
manner.

3. To surround for defense;
to fortify.

HEED *v.*
To mind; to regard with
care; to take notice of; to
attend to; to observe.

HEED *n.*
1. Caution; care; watch for
danger; notice; circum-
spection.

2. Notice; observation; regard; attention.

HEINOUS *a.*
Properly, hateful; odious;
great, enormous, aggra-
vated.

HEIR *n.*
1. The man who succeeds,
or is to succeed another in
the possession of lands,
tenements and heredita-
ments, by descent; the man
on whom the law casts an
estate of inheritance by the
death of the ancestor or
former possessor; the man
in whom the title to an estate of inheritance is vested
by the operation of law, on
the death of a former
owner.

2. One who inherits, or
takes from an ancestor.

3. One who succeeds to
the estate of a former possessor.

4. One who is entitled to possess.

HELL *n.*
1. The place or state of punishment for the wicked after death.
2. The place of the dead, or of souls after death; the lower regions, or the grave.

HELM *n.*
The instrument by which a ship is steered, consisting of a rudder, a tiller, and in large vessels, a wheel.

HELP *v.*
1. To aid; to assist; to lend strength or means towards effecting a purpose.
2. To assist; to succor; to lend means of deliverance.

HELP *n.*
1. Aid; assistance; strength or means furnished towards promoting an object, or deliverance from diffi-culty or distress.
2. That which gives assis-tance; he or that which contributes to advance a purpose.
3. Remedy; relief.

HELVE *n.*

The handle of an ax or hatchet.

HEMLOCK *n.*
A plant of the genus Conium, whose leaves and root are poisonous.

HENCE *adv.*
1. From this place.
2. From this time; in the future.
3. From this cause or rea-son, noting a consequence, inference or deduction from something just before stated.
4. From this source or original.

HENCEFORTH *adv.*
From this time forward.

HENCEFORWARD *adv.*
From this time forward; henceforth.

HERALD *n.*
1. An officer whose busi-ness was to denounce or proclaim war, to challenge to battle, to proclaim peace, and to bear mes-sages from the commander of an army.
2. A proclaimer; a pub-lisher.

HERB *n.*
A plant or vegetable with a soft or succulent stalk or stem, which dies to the root every year, and is thus distinguished from a tree and a shrub, which have ligneous or hard woody stems.

HEREAFTER *adv.*
In time to come; in some future time.

HEREBY *adv.*
By this.

HEREIN *adv.*
In this.

HEREOF *adv.*
Of this; from this.

HERESY *n.*
A fundamental error in religion, or an error of opinion respecting some fundamental doctrine of religion.

HERETICK *n.*
1. A person who holds and teaches opinions repugnant to the established faith; a person who holds and avows religious opinions contrary to the doctrines of Scripture, the only rule of faith and practice.
2. Any one who maintains erroneous opinions.

HERETOFORE *adv.*
In times before the present; formerly.

HEREUNTO *adv.*
To this.

HEREWITH *adv.*
With this.

HERITAGE *n.*
1. Inheritance; an estate that passes from an ancestor to an heir by descent or course of law; that which is inherited.
2. The saints or people of God are called his heritage, as being claimed by him, and the objects of his special care.

HERON *n.*
A large fowl of the genus Ardea, a great devourer of fish.

HEW *v.*
1. To cut with an ax, or other like instrument, for the purpose of making an even surface or side.
2. To chop; to cut; to hack.

3. To cut with a chisel; to make smooth.
4. To form or shape with an edged instrument.

HEWN *v.*
The same as hewed.

HIGHMINDED *a.*
Lofty in Mind; Arrogant.

HIGHWAY *n.*
1. A public road; a way open to all passengers.
2. Course; road; train of action.

HIN *n.*
A Hebrew measure of capacity containing the sixth part of an ephah, or about five quarts English measure.

HIND *n.*
The female of the red deer or stag.

HINDER *a.*
That is in a position contrary to that of the head or fore part; designating the part which follows.

HIRELING *n.*
One who is hired, or who serves for wages.

HISS *v.*
1. To make a sound by driving the breath between the tongue and the upper teeth; to give a strong aspiration, resembling the noise made by a serpent and some other animals, or that of water thrown on hot iron.
2. To express contempt or disapprobation by hissing.

HITHER *adv.*
1. To this place; used with verbs signifying motion.
2. Hither and thither, to this place and that.
3. To this point; to this argument or topic; to this end.

HITHERTO *adv.*
1. In any time, or every time till now; in time preceding the present.
2. To this place; to a prescribed limit.

HOAR *a.*
1. White.
2. Gray; white with age; hoary.

HOAR-FROST *n.*
The white particles of ice formed by the congelation

of dew or watery vapors.

HOARY *n.*
White or gray with age.

HOCK *n.*
The joint of an animal between the knee and the fetlock.

HOISE *v.*
To hoist.

HOLDEN *v.*
Held.

HOLILY *adv.*
1. Piously; with sanctity.
2. Sacredly; inviolably; without breach.

HOLINESS *n.*
1. The state of being holy; purity or integrity of moral character; freedom from sin; sanctity.
2. Purity of heart or dispositions; sanctified affections; piety; moral goodness.
3. Sacredness; the state of any thing hallowed, or consecrated to God or to his worship.
4. That which is separated to the service of God.

HOLPEN *past tense of help.*

HOLY *a.*
1. Properly, whole, entire or perfect.
2. Hallowed.
3. Perfectly just and good.
4. Sacred.

HOLYDAY *n.*
A day set apart for commemorating some important event in history; a festival intended to celebrate some event deemed auspicious to the welfare of a nation.

HOMEBORN *a.*
1. Native; natural.
2. Domestic; not foreign.

HOMER *n.*
A Hebrew measure containing the tenth part of an epha, or about six pints.

HONEST *a.*
1. Upright; just; fair in dealing with others; free from trickishness and fraud; acting and having the disposition to act at all times according to justice or correct moral principles.
2. Fair; just; equitable; free

from fraud.

3. Sincere; proceeding from pure or just principles, or directed to a good object.

4. Fair; good; unimpeached.

5. Decent; honorable; or suitable.

HONOUR *n.*

1. The esteem due or paid to worth; high estimation.

2. A testimony of esteem; any expression of respect or of high estimation by words or actions.

3. Dignity; exalted rank or place; distinction.

4. Reverence; veneration; or any act by which reverence and submission are expressed.

5. Reputation; good name.

6. True nobleness of mind; magnanimity; dignified respect for character, springing from probity, principle or moral rectitude.

HONOR *v.*

1. To revere; to respect; to treat with deference and submission, and perform relative duties to.

2. To reverence; to mani-fest the highest veneration for, in words and actions; to entertain the most exalted thoughts of; to worship; to adore.

3. To dignify; to raise to distinction or notice; to elevate in rank or station; to exalt.

4. To glorify; to render illustrious.

HOPE *n.*

1. A desire of some good, accompanied with at least a slight expectation of obtaining it, or a belief that it is obtainable.

2. Confidence in a future event; the highest degree of well founded expectation of good.

3. That which gives hope; he or that which furnishes ground of expectation, or promises desired good.

4. An opinion or belief not amounting to certainty, but grounded on substantial evidence.

HOPE *v.*

1. To cherish a desire of good, with some expectation of obtaining it, or a belief that it is obtainable.

2. To place confidence in;

to trust in with confident expectation of good.

HOSANNA *n.*
An exclamation of praise to God, or an invocation of blessings.

HOSEN *n.*
1. Breeches or trowsers.
2. Stockings; coverings for the legs.

HOSPITALITY *n.*
The act or practice of receiving and entertaining strangers or guests without reward, or with kind and generous liberality.

HOUGH *n.*
1. The lower part of the thigh; the ham; the joint of the hind leg of a beast that connects the thigh with the leg.
2. An adz; a hoe.

HOUGH *v.*
To hamstring; to disable by cutting the sinews of the ham.

HOWBEIT *adv.*
Be it as it may; nevertheless; notwithstanding; yet; but; however.

HOWSOEVER *adv.*
1. In what manner soever.
2. Although.

HUMBLE *a.*
1. Low.
2. Mean; not magnificent.
3. Lowly; modest; meek; submissive; opposed to proud, haughty, arrogant or assuming.

HUMBLE *v.*
1. To abase; to reduce to a low state.
2. To crush; to break; to subdue.
3. To mortify.
4. To make humble or lowly in mind; to abase the pride of; to reduce arrogance and self-dependence; to give a low opinion of one's moral worth; to make meek and submissive to the divine will.
5. To make to condescend.
6. To bring down; to lower; to reduce.
7. To deprive of chastity.

HUMILITY *n.*
1. Freedom from pride and arrogance; humbleness of mind; a modest estimate of one's own worth.

2. Lowliness of mind; a deep sense of one's own unworthiness in the sight of God, self-abasement, penitence for sin, and submission to the divine will.
3. Act of submission.

HUNGRED *a.*
Hungry; pinched by want of food.

HUSBANDMAN *n.*
1. A farmer; a cultivator or tiller of the ground; one who labors in tillage.
2. The master of a family.

HUSBANDRY *n.*
The business of a farmer, comprehending agriculture or tillage of the ground, the raising, managing and fattening of cattle and other domestic animals, the management of the dairy and whatever the land produces.

HUSK *n.*
The external covering of certain fruits or seeds of plants.

HYMN *n.*
A short poem, composed for religious service, or a song of joy and praise to God.

HYPOCRISY *n.*
1. Simulation; a feigning to be what one is not; or dissimulation, a concealment of one's real character or motives.
2. Assuming of a false appearance of virtue or religion; a deceitful show of a good character; a counterfeiting of religion.

HYPOCRITE *n.*
1. One who feigns to be what he is not; one who has the form of godliness without the power, or who assumes an appearance of piety and virtue, when he is destitute of true religion.
2. A dissembler; one who assumes a false appearance.

HYSSOP *n.*
A plant or genus of plants, one species of which is cultivated for use.

IDLE *a.*
1. Not employed; unoccupied with business; inactive; doing nothing.
2. Slothful; given to rest

and ease; averse to labor or employment.

3. Unfruitful; barren; not productive of good.

4. Unprofitable; not tending to edification.

IDOL *n.*

1. An image, form or representation, usually of a man or other animal, consecrated as an object of worship; a pagan deity.

2. Any thing on which we set our affections; that to which we indulge an excessive and sinful attachment.

IDOLATER *n.*

A worshiper of idols; one who pays divine honors to images, statues, or representations of any thing made by hands; one who worships as a deity that which is not God; a pagan.

IGNOMINY *n.*

Public disgrace; shame; reproach; dishonor; infamy.

IGNORANCE *n.*

Want, absence or destitution of knowledge; the negative state of the mind which has not been instructed in arts, literature or science, or has not been informed of facts.

ILLUMINATE *v.*

1. To enlighten; to throw light on; to supply with light.

2. To enlighten intellectually with knowledge or grace.

3. To adorn with pictures, portraits and other paintings.

ILLUMINATE *a.*

Enlightened.

IMMORTAL *a.*

1. Having no principle of alteration or corruption; exempt from death; having life or being that shall never end.

2. Never ending; everlasting; continual.

3. Perpetual; having unlimited existence.

4. Destined to live in all the ages of this world; imperishable.

IMMORTALITY *n.*

The quality of never ceasing to live or exist; exemption from death and annihilation; life destined to endure without end.

IMMUTABLE *a.*
Invariable; unalterable; not capable or susceptible of change.

IMPART *v.*
To give, grant or communicate; to bestow on another a share or portion of something.

IMPEDIMENT *n.*
That which prevents distinct articulation.

IMPENITANT *a.*
Not penitent; not repenting of sin; not contrite; obdurate; of a hard heart.

IMPERIOUS *a.*
Commanding; dictatorial; haughty; arrogant; overbearing; domineering.

IMPLACABLE *a.*
1. Not to be appeased; that can not be pacified and rendered peaceable; inexorable; stubborn or constant in enmity.
2. Not to be appeased or subdued.

IMPLEAD *v.*
To institute and prosecute a suit against one in court; to sue at law.

IMPORTUNITY *n.*
Pressing solicitation; urgent request; application for a claim or favor, which is urged with troublesome frequency or pertinacity.

IMPOSE *v.*
1. To lay on; to set on; to lay on.
2. To lay on, as a command; to enjoin, as a duty.

IMPOTENT *a.*
Weak; feeble; wanting strength or power; unable by nature, or disabled by disease or accident to perform any act.

IMPOVERISH *v.*
1. To make poor; to reduce to poverty or indigence.
2. To exhaust strength, richness or fertility.

IMPUDENT *a.*
Shameless; wanting modesty; bold with contempt of others; saucy.

IMPUTE *v.*

1. To charge; to attribute; to set to the account of.
2. To attribute; to ascribe.
3. To reckon to one what does not belong to him.

INASMUCH *adv.* (1913)
In like degree; in like manner; seeing that; considering that; since.

INCLINE *v.*
1. To lean; to deviate from an erect or parallel line toward any object; to tend.
2. To lean; in a moral sense; to have a propension; to be disposed; to have some wish or desire.
3. To give a tendency or propension to the will or affections; to turn; to dispose.

INCLOSE *v.*
To surround; to shut in; to confine on all sides.

INCONTINENT *a.*
Not restraining the passions or appetites.

INCORRUPTION *n.*
Incapacity of being corrupted.

INDIGNATION *n.*

1. Anger or extreme anger, mingled with contempt, disgust or abhorrence.
2. The anger of a superior; extreme anger; particularly, the wrath of God against sinful men for their ingratitude and rebellion.
3. The effects of anger; the dreadful effects of God's wrath; terrible judgments.
4. Holy displeasure at one's self for sin.

INDITING *ppr.*
Committing to words in writing; dictating what shall be written.

INDUSTRIOUS *a.*
Diligent in business or study; constantly, regularly or habitually occupied in business; assiduous; opposed to slothful and idle.

INFAMOUS *a.*
Of ill report, emphatically; having a reputation of the worst kind; publicly branded with odium for vice of guilt; base; scandalous; notoriously vile.

INFAMY *n.*
1. Total loss of reputation; public disgrace.

2. Qualities which are detested and despised; qualities notoriously bad and scandalous.

INFIDEL *a.*
Unbelieving; disbelieving the inspiration of the Scriptures, or the divine institution of Christianity.

INFIDEL *n.*
One who disbelieves the inspiration of the Scriptures, and the divine origin of Christianity.

INFINITE *a.*
1. Without limits; unbounded; boundless; not circumscribed; applied to time, space and qualities.
2. That will have no end.
3. That has a beginning in space, but is infinitely extended.

INFIRMITY *n.*
1. An unsound or unhealthy state of the body; weakness; feebleness.
2. Weakness of mind; failing; fault; foible.
3. Weakness of resolution.
4. Any particular disease; malady.
5. Defect; imperfection; weakness.

INFOLDING *v.*
Involving; wrapping up; clasping.

INGATHERING *n.*
The act or business of collecting and securing the fruits of the earth; harvest.

INHERIT *v.*
1. To possess; to enjoy; to take as a possession, by gift or divine appropriation.
2. To take by descent from an ancestor; to take by succession; to receive, as a right or title descendible by law from an ancestor at his decease.
3. To receive by nature from a progenitor.

INIQUITY *n.*
1. Injustice; unrighteousness; a deviation from rectitude.
2. Want of rectitude in principle.
3. A particular deviation from rectitude; a sin or crime; wickedness; any act of injustice.

INJUSTICE *n.*

1. Iniquity; wrong; any violation of another's rights; the withholding of what is due.
2. The withholding from another merited praise, or ascribing to him unmerited blame.

INORDINATE *a.*
Irregular; disorderly; excessive; immoderate; not limited to rules prescribed, or to usual bounds.

INQUISITION *n.*
1. Inquiry; examination; a searching or search.
2. Judicial inquiry; official examination; inquest.

INSCRIPTION *n.*
Something written or engraved to communicate knowledge to after ages; any character, word, line or sentence written or engraved on a solid substance for duration.

INSOMUCH *adv.*
So that; to that degree.

INSTANT *a.*
Pressing; urgent; importunate; earnest.

INSTANT *n.*
A point in duration; a moment; a part of duration in which we perceive no succession, or a part that occupies the time of a single thought.

INSURRECTION *n.*
1. A rising against civil or political authority; the open and active opposition of a number of persons to the execution of a law in a city or state.
2. A rising in mass to oppose an enemy.

INTERCESSION *n.*
The act of interceding; mediation; interposition between parties at variance, with a view to reconciliation; prayer or solicitation to one party in favor of another, sometimes against another.

INTERMEDDLE *v.*
To meddle in the affairs of others, in which one has no concern; to meddle officiously; to interpose or interfere improperly.

INTERPRET *v.*
1. To explain the meaning

or words to a person who does not understand them; to expound; to translate unintelligible words into intelligible ones.

2. To explain or unfold the meaning of predictions, vision, dreams or enigmas; to expound and lay open what is concealed from the understanding.

3. To decipher.

4. To explain something not understood.

5. To define; to explain words by other words in the same language.

INTREAT *v.*
1. To make an earnest petition or request.
2. To offer a treaty.
3. To treat; to discourse.

ISLE *n.*
A tract of land surrounded by water, or a detached portion of land embosomed in the ocean, in a lake or river.

ISSUE *n.*
1. The act of passing or flowing out; a moving out of any inclosed place; egress.
2. Evacuation; discharge; a flux or running.

JANGLING *v.*
Wrangling; quarreling; sounding discordantly.

JEALOUSY *n.*
1. That passion of peculiar uneasiness which arises from the fear that a rival may rob us of the affection of one whom we love, or the suspicion that he has already done it.
2. The uneasiness which arises from the fear that another does or will enjoy some advantage which we desire for ourselves.
3. Suspicious fear or apprehension.
4. Suspicious caution or vigilance, an earnest concern or solicitude for the welfare or honor of others.
5. Indignation.

JEHOVAH *n.*
The Scripture name of the Supreme Being.

JEHOVAH-JIREH
(Strongs)
Jehovah will see.

JEHOVAH-NISSE
(Strongs)

Jehovah is my banner.

JEHOVAH-SHALOM
(Strongs)
Jehovah is peace.

JEOPARDY *n.*
Exposure to death, loss or injury; hazard; danger; peril.

JESTING *v.*
Joking; talking for diversion or merriment.

JESUS *n.*
The Savior; the name of the Son of God as announced by the angel to his parents; the personal name of Our Lord, in distinction from Christ, his official appellation.

JEW *n.*
A Hebrew or Israelite.

JEWRY *n.*
Judea.

JOT *n.*
An iota; a point; a tittle; the least quantity assignable.

JOY *n.*
1. The passion or emotion excited by the acquisition or expectation of good; that excitement of pleasurable feelings which is caused by success, good fortune, the gratification of desire or some good possessed, or by a rational prospect of possessing what we love or desire; gladness; exultation; exhilaration of spirits.
2. A glorious and triumphant state.
3. The cause of joy or happiness.

JOY *v.*
To rejoice; to be glad; to exult.

JUBILEE *n.*
Among the Jews, every fiftieth year, being the year following the revolution of seven weeks of years, at which time all the slaves were liberated, and all lands which had been alienated during the whole period, reverted to their former owners.

JUDGE *n.*
1. A civil officer who is invested with authority to hear and determine causes,

civil or criminal, between parties, according to his commission.

2. The Supreme Being.

3. One who presides in a court of judicature.

4. One who has skill to decide on the merits of a question, or on the value of any thing; one who can discern truth and propriety.

5. A chief magistrate, with civil and military powers.

JUDGE *v.*

1. To compare facts or ideas, and perceive their agreement or disagreement, and thus to distinguish truth from falsehood.

2. To form an opinion; to bring to issue the reasoning or deliberations of the mind.

3. To hear and determine; to pass sentence.

4. To discern; to distinguish; to consider accurately for the purpose of forming an opinion or conclusion.

5. To try; to examine and pass sentence on.

6. To rule or govern.

JUDGMENT *n.*

1. The act or process of the mind in comparing its ideas, to find their agreement or disagreement, and to ascertain truth; or the process of examining facts and arguments, to ascertain propriety and justice; or the process of examining the relations between one proposition and another.

2. The faculty of the mind by which man is enabled to compare ideas and ascertain the relations of terms and propositions.

3. The determination of the mind, formed from comparing the relations of ideas, or the comparison of facts and arguments.

4. In law, the sentence of doom pronounced in any cause, civil or criminal, by the judge or court by which it is tried.

5. The right or power of passing sentence.

6. Determination; decision.

7. Opinion; notion.

8. The spirit of wisdom and prudence, enabling a person to discern right and wrong, good and evil.

9. A remarkable punishment; an extraordinary calamity inflicted by God on sinners.

10. The spiritual government of the world.

11. The doctrines of the gospel, or God's word.

12. Justice and equity.

13. The decrees and purposes of God concerning nations.

14. The gospel, or kingdom of grace.

15. The final trial of the human race, when God will decide the fate of every individual, and award sentence according to justice.

JURISDICTION *n.*
The legal power of authority of doing justice in cases of complaint; the power of executing the laws and distributing justice.

JUST *a.*
1. Regular; orderly; due; suitable.

2. Exactly proportioned; proper.

3. Full; complete to the common standard.

4. Upright; honest; having principles of rectitude; or conforming exactly to the laws, and to principles of rectitude in social conduct; equitable in the distribution of justice.

5. Righteous; religious; influenced by a regard to the laws of God; or living in exact conformity to the divine will.

6. Conformed to rules of justice; doing equal justice.

7. Conformed to truth; exact; proper; accurate; just expressions; just images or representations.

8. True; founded in truth and fact.

9. Innocent; blameless; without guilt.

10. Equitable; due; merited.

11. Impartial; allowing what is due; giving fair representation of character, merit or demerit.

JUSTICE *n.*
1. The virtue which consists in giving to every one what is his due; practical conformity to the laws and to principles of rectitude in the dealings of men with each other; honesty; integrity in commerce or mutual intercourse.

2. Impartiality; equal distribution of right in expressing opinions; fair representation of facts re-

specting merit or demerit.
3. Equity; agreeableness to right.
4. Vindictive retribution; merited punishment.
5. Right; application of equity.

JUSTIFICATION *n.*

1. The act of justifying; a showing to be just or conformable to law, rectitude or propriety; vindication; defense.
2. Absolution.
3. Remission of sin and absolution from guilt and punishment; an act of free grace by which God pardons the sinner and accepts him as righteous, on account of the atonement of Christ.

JUSTIFY *v.*

1. To prove or show to be just, or conformable to law, right, justice, propriety or duty; to defend or maintain; to vindicate as right.
2. To pardon and clear form guilt; to absolve or acquit from guilt and merited punishment, and to accept as righteous on account of the merits of the

Savior, or by the application of Christ's atonement to the offender.
3. To cause another to appear comparatively righteous, or less guilty than one's self.
4. To judge rightly of.
5. To accept as just and treat with favor.

JUSTLE *v.*

To run against; to encounter; to strike against; to clash.

KERCHIEF *n.*

1. A head dress; a cloth to cover the head.
2. A cloth used in dress.

KERNEL *n.*

The central part of any thing; a small mass around which other matter is concreted; a nucleus.

KETTLE *n.*

A vessel of iron or other metal, with a wide mouth, usually without a cover, used for heating and boiling water or other liquor.

KID *n.*

A young goat.

KIN *n.*
Relatives; kindred; persons of the same race.

KIND *a.*
Disposed to do good to others, and to make them happy by granting their requests, supplying their wants or assisting them in distress; having tenderness or goodness of nature; benevolent; benignant.

KINDLE *v.*
1. To set on fire; to cause to burn with flame; to light.
2. To inflame, as the passions; to exasperate; to rouse; to provoke; to excite to action; to heat; to fire; to animate,
3. To bring forth.
4. To begin to rage, or be violently excited; to be roused or exasperated.

KINDNESS *n.*
1. Good will; benevolence; that temper or disposition which delights in contributing to the happiness of others, which is exercised cheerfully in gratifying their wishes, supplying their wants or alleviating their distresses; benignity of nature.
2. Act of good will; beneficence; any act of benevolence which promotes the happiness or welfare of others.

KINDRED *n.*
1. Relation by birth; consanguinity.
2. Relation by marriage; affinity.
3. Relatives by blood or marriage, more properly the former.

KINDRED *a.*
Related; congenial; of the like nature or properties.

KINE *plural of cow.*

KING *n.*
1. The chief or sovereign of a nation; a man invested with supreme authority over a nation, tribe or country; a monarch.
2. A sovereign; a prince; a ruler.

KINGDOM *n.*
1. The territory or country subject to a king; an undivided territory under the dominion of a king or

monarch.

2. The inhabitants or population subject to a king.

3. The government or universal dominion of God.

4. The power of supreme administration.

5. A princely nation or state.

6. Heaven.

7. State of glory in heaven.

8. The reign of the Messiah.

9. Government; rule; supreme administration.

KINSFOLK *n.*
Relations; kindred; persons of the same family.

KINSMAN *n.*
A man of the same race or family; one related by blood.

KINSWOMAN *n.*
A female relation.

KITE *n.*
A rapacious fowl of the genus Falco or hawk, remarkable for gliding through the air without frequently moving its wings.

KNEW *past tense of know.*

KNOP *n.*

A knob; a tufted top; a bud; a bunch; a button.

KNOW *v.*
1. To perceive with certainty; to understand clearly; to have a clear and certain perception of truth, fact, or any thing that actually exists.

2. To be informed of; to be taught.

3. To distinguish.

4. To recognize by recollection, remembrance, representation or description.

5. To be no stranger to; to be familiar.

6. To have sexual commerce with.

7. To approve.

8. To learn.

9. To acknowledge with due respect.

10. To choose; to favor or take an interest in.

11. To commit; to have.

12. To have full assurance of; to have satisfactory evidence of any thing, though short of certainty.

KNOWLEDGE *n.*
1. A clear and certain perception of that which exists, or of truth and fact; the perception of the con-

nection and agreement, or disagreement and repugnancy of our ideas.
2. Learning; illumination of mind.
3. Skill.
4. Acquaintance with any fact or person.
5. Cognizance; notice.
6. Information; power of knowing.
7. Sexual intercourse.

LAD *n.*
A young man or boy; a stripling.

LADE *v.*
1. To load; to put on or in.
2. To dip; to throw in or out.

LADEN *v.*
1. Loaded; charged with a burden or freight.
2. Oppressed; burdened.

LAIN *v. of lie.*

LAME *a.*
1. Crippled or disabled in a limb, or otherwise injured so as to be unsound and impaired in strength.
2. Imperfect; not satisfactory.

LAMENT *v.*
1. To mourn; to grieve; to weep or wail; to express sorrow.
2. To regret deeply; to feel sorrow.

LAMENTATION *n.*
Expression of sorrow; cries of grief; the act of bewailing. Expression of sorrow; cries of grief; the act of bewailing.

LANCE *n.*
A spear, an offensive weapon in form of a half pike, used by the ancients and thrown by the hand. It consisted of the shaft or handle, the wings and the dart.

LANCET *n.*
A surgical instrument, sharp-pointed and two-edged; used in venesection, and in opening tumors, abscesses, &c.

LANDMARK *n.*
A mark to designate the boundary of land; any mark or fixed object.

LANGUISH *v.*
1. To lose strength or ani-

mation; to be or become dull, feeble or spiritless; to pine; to be or to grow heavy.

2. To wither; to fade; to lose the vegetating power.

LAP *n.*
The part of clothes that lies on the knees when a person sits down; the knees in this position.

LAP *v.*
To take into the mouth with the tongue; to lick up.

LAPWING *n.*
A bird of the genus Tringa; the tewit.

LASCIVIOUSNESS *n.*
1. Looseness; irregular indulgence of animal desires; wantonness; lustfulness.
2. Tendency to excite lust, and promote irregular indulgences.

LATCHET *n.*
The string that fastens a shoe.

LATTER *a.*
1. Coming or happening after something else.
2. Mentioned the last of

two.
3. Modern; lately done or past.

LAUD *n.*
1. Praise; commendation; an extolling in words; honorable mention.
2. That part of divine worship which consists in praise.

LAVER *n.*
A vessel for washing; a large basin; in scripture history, a basin placed in the court of the Jewish tabernacle, where the officiating priests washed their hands and feet and the entrails of victims.

LAVISH *a.*
1. Prodigal; expending or bestowing with profusion; profuse.
2. Wasteful; expending without necessity; liberal to a fault.
3. Wild; unrestrained.

LAWYER *n.*
One versed in the laws, or a practitioner of law; one whose profession is to institute suits in courts of law, and to prosecute or

defend the cause of clients.

LEAGUE *n.*
A combination or union of two or more parties for the purpose of maintaining friendship and promoting their mutual interest, or for executing any design in concert.

LEASING *n.*
Falsehood; lies.

LEATHERN *a.*
Made of leather; consisting of leather.

LEAVEN *n.*
1. A mass of sour dough, which, mixed with a larger quantity of dough or paste, produces fermentation in it and renders it light.
2. Any thing which makes a general change in the mass.

LEAVEN *v.*
1. To excite fermentation in; to raise and make light.
2. To taint; to imbue.

LEEK *n.*
A plant of the genus Allium, with a bulbous root.

LEES *n.*
The grosser parts of any liquor which have settled on the bottom of a vessel; dregs; sediment.

LEGION *n.*
1. In Roman antiquity, a body of infantry consisting of different numbers of men at different periods, from three to five thousand.
2. A military force; military bands.
3. A great number.

LEISURE *n.*
1. Freedom from occupation or business; vacant time; time free from employment.
2. Convenience of time.

LEND *v.*
To grant to another for temporary use, on the express or implied condition that the thing shall be returned.

LENT *v. of lend.*

LEPROSY *n.*
A foul cutaneous disease, appearing in dry, white, thin, scurfy scabs, attended

with violent itching.

LEST *con.*
That not; for fear that.

LET *v.*
1. To retard; to hinder; to impede; to interpose obstructions.
2. To forbear.

LEVIATHAN *n.*
An aquatic animal; the crooked serpent.

LEVY *v.*
1. To raise; to collect.
2. To raise; to collect by assessment.

LEVY *n.*
The act of collecting men for military, or other public service, as by enlistment, enrollment or other means.

LEWD *a.*
1. Given to the unlawful indulgence of lust; addicted to fornication or adultery; dissolute; lustful; libidinous.
2. Proceeding from unlawful lust.
3. Wicked; vile; profligate; licentious.

LIAR *n.*
1. A person who knowingly utters falsehood; one who declares to another as a fact what he knows to be not true, and with an intention to deceive him.
2. One who denies Christ.

LIBERAL *a.*
1. Of a free heart; free to give or bestow; not close or contracted; munificent; bountiful; generous; giving largely.
2. Generous; ample; large.
3. Not selfish; enlarged; embracing other interests than one's own.

LIBERTY *n.*
1. Freedom from restraint, in a general sense, and applicable to the body, or to the will or mind.
2. Natural liberty, consists in the power of acting as one thinks fit, without any restraint or control, except from the laws of nature.
3. Freedom of the will; exemption from compulsion or restraint in willing or volition.

LICENCE *n.*
To permit by grant of au-

thority or liberty given to do or forbear any act.

LIE *n.*
A criminal falsehood; a falsehood uttered for the purpose of deception; an intentional violation of truth.

LIE *v.*
1. To utter falsehood with an intention to deceive, or with an immoral design.
2. To exhibit a false representation; to say or do that which deceives another, when he has a right to know the truth, or when morality requires a just representation.

LIKEN *v.*
To compare; to represent as resembling or similar.

LINEAGE *n.*
Race; progeny; descendants in a line from a common progenitor.

LINGER *v.*
1. To delay; to loiter; to remain or wait long; to be slow.
2. To hesitate; to be slow in deciding; to be in suspense.
3. To remain long in any state.

LISTETH *v.*
To Wish; To be inclined to.

LITTER *n.*
A vehicle formed with shafts supporting a bed between them, in which a person may be borne by men or by a horse.

LIVELY *a.*
1. Brisk; vigorous; vivacious; active; as a lively youth.
2. Strong; energetic.

LO *exclam.*
Look; see; behold; observe.

LOATHE *v.*
To hate; to look on with hatred or abhorrence.

LOCK *n.*
A tuft of hair; a plexus of wool, hay or other like substance; a flock; a ringlet of hair.

LOFT *n.*
1. An elevation.

2. A high room or place.

LOFTY *a.*
1. Elevated in place; high.
2. Elevated in condition or character.
3. Proud; haughty.

LOINS *n.*
The space on each side of the vertebrae, between the lowest of the false ribs and the upper portion of the os ilium or haunch bone, or the lateral portions of the lumbar region; reins.

LONG *v.*
To desire earnestly or eagerly.

LONGSUFFERING *n.*
Long endurance; patience of offense.

LOOSE *v.*
1. To untie or unbind; to free from any fastening.
2. To relax.
3. To release from imprisonment; to liberate; to set at liberty.
4. To free from obligation.
5. To relieve; to free from any thing burdensome or afflictive.
6. To put off.

7. To open.
8. To remit; to absolve.
9. To set sail; to leave a port or harbor.

LOP *v.*
To cut off, as the top or extreme part of any thing; to shorten by cutting off the extremities.

LORD *n.*
1. The Supreme Being; Jehovah.
2. A husband.
3. A master; a person possessing supreme power and authority; a ruler; a governor.
4. A tyrant; an oppressive ruler.

LORD *v.*
To domineer; to rule with arbitrary or despotic sway.

LORDSHIP *n.*
1. The state of quality of being a lord.
2. Dominion; power; authority.
3. Seigniory; domain; the territory of a lord over which he holds jurisdiction; a manor.

LOT *n.*

1. That which, in human speech, is called chance, hazard, fortune; but in strictness of language, is the determination of Providence.

2. That by which the fate or portion of one is determined; that by which an event is committed to chance, that is, to the determination of Providence.

3. The part, division or fate which falls to one by chance, that is, by divine determination.

LOTHE *v.*

To hate; to look on with hatred or abhorrence; particularly, to feel disgust at food or drink, either from natural antipathy, or a sickly appetite, or from satiety, or from its ill taste.

LOVE *v.*

1. To be pleased with; to regard with affection, on account of some qualities which excite pleasing sensations or desire of gratification.

2. To have benevolence or good will for.

LOVE *n.*

1. An affection of the mind excited by beauty and worth of any kind, or by the qualities of an object which communicate pleasure, sensual or intellectual.

2. Benevolence; good will.

LOVINGKINDNESS *n.*

Tender regard; mercy; favor.

LOWLINESS *n.*

1. Freedom from pride; humility; humbleness of mind.

2. Meanness; want of dignity; abject state.

LOWLY *a.*

1. Having a low esteem of one's own worth; humble; meek; free from pride.

2. Mean; low; wanting dignity or rank.

3. Not high; not elevated in place.

LUCRE *n.*

Gain in money or goods; profit.

LUKEWARM *a.*

Not ardent; not zealous; cool; indifferent.

LUNATICK *n.*

A person affected by insanity, supposed to be influenced or produced by the moon or its position in orbit; a madman.

LURK *v.*
1. To lie hid; to lie in wait.
2. To lie concealed or unperceived.

LUST *n.*
1. Longing desire; eagerness to possess or enjoy.
2. Concupiscence; carnal appetite; unlawful desire of carnal pleasure.
3. Evil propensity; depraved affections and desires.

LUST *v.*
1. To desire eagerly; to long; with after.
2. To have carnal desire; to desire eagerly the gratification of carnal appetite.
3. To have irregular or inordinate desires.
4. To list; to like.

MAD *a.*
1. Disordered in intellect; distracted; furious.
2. Proceeding from disordered intellect or expressing it.

3. Enraged; furious.
4. Inflamed to excess with desire; excited with violent and unreasonable passion or appetite; infatuated.
5. Distracted with anxiety or trouble; extremely perplexed.
6. Infatuated with folly.

MAGICIAN *n.*
One skilled in magic; one that practices the black art; an enchanter; a necromancer; a sorcerer or sorceress.

MAGNIFY *v.*
1. To make great or greater; to increase the apparent dimensions of a body.
2. To make great in representation; to extol; to exalt in description or praise.
3. To extol; to exalt; to elevate; to raise in estimation.

MAID *n.*
A species of skate fish.

MAIDEN *n.*
1. An unmarried woman, or a young unmarried woman; a virgin.
2. A female servant.

MAIM *v.*

1. To deprive of the use of a limb, so as to render a person less able to defend himself in fighting, or to annoy his adversary.
2. To deprive of a necessary part; to cripple; to disable.

MAJESTY *n.*
1. Greatness of appearance; dignity; grandeur; dignity of aspect or manner; the quality or state of a person or thing which inspires awe or reverence in the beholder.
2. Dignity; elevation of manner.

MALEFACTOR *n.*
One who commits a crime; one guilty of violating the laws, in such a manner as to subject him to public prosecution and punishment, particularly to capital punishment; a criminal.

MALICE *n.*
Extreme enmity of heart, or malevolence; a disposition to injure others without cause, from mere personal gratification or from a spirit of revenge; unprovoked malignity or spite.

MALICE *v.*
To regard with extreme ill will.

MALICIOUS *a.*
1. Harboring ill will or enmity without provocation; malevolent in the extreme; malignant in heart.
2. Proceeding from extreme hatred or ill will; dictated by malice.

MALIGNITY *n.*
Extreme enmity, or evil dispositions of heart towards another; malice without provocation, or malevolence with baseness of heart; deep rooted spite.

MALLOW *n.*
A plant of the genus Malva.

MAMMON *n.*
Riches; wealth; or the god or riches.

MAN *n.*
1. Mankind; the human race; the whole species of human beings; beings distinguished from all other animals by the powers of reason and speech, as well as by their shape and dig-

nified aspect.
2. A male individual of the human race, of adult growth or years.

MANDRAKE *n.*
A plant of the genus Atroopa; a narcotic.

MANGER *n.*
A trough or box in which fodder is laid for cattle, or the place in which horses and cattle are fed.

MANIFEST *a.*
Plain, open, clearly visible to the eye or obvious to the understanding; apparent; not obscure or difficult to be seen or understood.

MANIFOLD *a.*
1. Of divers kinds; many in number; numerous; multiplied.
2. Exhibited or appearing at divers times or in various ways.

MANNA *n.*
A substance miraculously furnished as food for the Israelites in their journey through the wilderness of Arabia.

MANNER *n.*
1. Form; method; way of performing or executing.
2. Custom; habitual practice.
3. Sort; kind.
4. Certain degree or measure.

MANSION *n.*
Any place of residence; a house; a habitation.

MANSLAYER *n.*
One that has slain a human being.

MANTLE *n.*
1. A kind of cloke or loose garment to be worn over other garments.
2. A cover; that which conceals.

MARANATHA *n.*
The Lord comes or has come.

MARISHE *n.*
Low ground, wet or covered with water and coarse grass; a fen; a bog; a moor.

MAR *v.*
1. To injure by cutting off a part, or by wounding and making defective.

2. To deform; to disfigure.

MARRIAGE *n.*
1. The act of uniting a man and woman for life; wedlock; the legal union of a man and woman for life.
2. The union between Christ and his church by the covenant of grace.

MARROW *n.*
1. A soft oleaginous substance contained in the cavities of animal bones.
2. The essence; the best part.

MARRY *v.*
1. To unite in wedlock or matrimony; to join a man and woman for life, and constitute them man and wife according to the laws or customs of a nation.
2. To unite in covenant, or in the closest connection.

MART *n.*
A place of sale or traffick.

MARTYR *n.*
One who, by his death, bears witness to the truth of the gospel.

MARVEL *n.*

1. A wonder; that which arrests the attention and causes a person to stand or gaze, or to pause.
2. Wonder; admiration.

MARVEL *v.*
To wonder.

MARVELLOUS *a.*
Wonderful; strange; exciting wonder or some degree of surprise.

MASCHIL *n.* (Strongs)
A didactive poem.

MASON *n.*
A man whose occupation is to lay bricks and stones, or to construct the walls of buildings, chimneys and the like, which consist of bricks or stones.

MASTERY *n.*
1. Dominion; power of governing or commanding.
2. Superiority in competition; preeminence.

MATE *n.*
A companion; an associate; one who customarily associates with another.

MATRIX *n.*

1. The womb; the cavity in which the fetus of an animal is formed and nourished till its birth.

2. A mold; the cavity in which any thing is formed, and which gives it shape.

MATTOCK *n.*

A tool to grub up weeds or roots; a grubbing hoe.

MAUL *n.*

A heavy wooden hammer.

MAW *n.*

The stomach of brutes.

MEAN *a.*

1. Wanting dignity; low in rank or birth.

2. Wanting dignity of mind; low minded; base; destitute of honor; spiritless.

3. Contemptible; despicable.

4. Of little value; low in worth or estimation; worthy of little or no regard.

MEASURE *n.*

1. The whole extent or dimensions of a thing, including length, breadth and thickness.

2. That by which extent or dimension is ascertained, either length, breadth, thickness, capacity, or amount.

3. Determined extent or length; limit.

4. A rule by which any thing is adjusted or proportioned.

5. Proportion; quantity settled.

6. Extent of power or office.

MEAT *n.*

1. Food in general; any thing eaten for nourishment, either by man or beast.

2. Spiritual food; that which sustains and nourishes spiritual life or holiness.

3. Spiritual comfort; that which delights the soul.

4. The more abstruse doctrines of the gospel, or mysteries of religion.

5. Ceremonial ordinances.

MEDDLE *v.*

1. To have to do; to take part; to interpose and act in the concerns of others, or in affairs in which one's interposition is not necessary; often with the sense

of intrusion or officiousness.

2. To have to do; to touch;
to handle.

MEDIA (1913) *plural of
medium*

MEDIAN *a.* (1913)
Being in the middle; run-
ning through the middle.

MEDIATOR *n.*
1. One that interposes between parties at variance
for the purpose of reconciling them.
2. By way of eminence,
Christ is the mediator, the
divine intercessor through
whom sinners may be rec-
onciled to an offended
God.

MEDITATE *v.*
1. To dwell on any thing in
thought; to contemplate; to
study; to turn or revolve
any subject in the mind.
2. To intend; to have in
contemplation.

MEDITATION *n.*
Close or continued
thought; the turning or re-
volving of a subject in the
mind; serious contempla-
tion.

MEEK *a.*
1. Mild of temper; soft;
gentle; not easily provoked
or irritated; yielding; given
to forbearance under injuries.
2. Humble; submissive to
the divine will; not proud,
self-sufficient or refractory; not peevish and apt to
complain of divine dispen-
sations.

MEET *a.*
Fit; suitable; proper; qualified; convenient; adapted,
as to a use or purpose.

MEMBER *n.*
A limb of animal bodies; a
subordinate part of the
main body.

MEND *v.*
1. To repair; to supply a
part broken or defective.
2. To correct; to set right;
to alter for the better.
3. To repair; to restore to a
sound state.

MENSTRUOUS *a.*
1. Having the monthly
flow or discharge.
2. Pertaining to the

monthly flow of females.

MERCHANDISE *n.*
1. The objects of commerce; wares, goods, commodities, whatever is usually bought or sold in trade.
2. Trade; traffick; commerce.

MERCHANT *n.*
A man who trafficks or carries on trade with foreign countries, or who exports and imports goods and sells them by wholesale.

MERCIFUL *a.*
1. Having or exercising mercy; compassionate; tender; disposed to pity offenders and to forgive their offenses; unwilling to punish for injuries.
2. Compassionate; tender; unwilling to give pain; not cruel.

MERCY *n.*
1. That benevolence, mildness or tenderness of heart which disposes a person to overlook injuries, or to treat an offender better than he deserves; the disposition that tempers justice, and induces an injured person to forgive trespasses and injuries, and to forbear punishment, or inflict less than law or justice will warrant.
2. An act or exercise of mercy or favor.
3. Pity; compassion manifested towards a person in distress.
4. Grace; favor.

MERCYSEAT *n.*
The propitiatory; the covering of the ark of the covenant among the Jews.

MERRILY *adv.*
With mirth; with gayety and laughter; jovially.

MERRY *a.*
1. Gay and noisy; jovial; exhilarated to laughter.
2. Causing laughter or mirth.
3. Pleasant; agreeable; delightful.

MESS *n.*
A dish or a quantity of food prepared or set on a table at one time.

MESSIAH *a.*

Christ, the anointed; the Savior of the world.

METE *v.*
To measure; to ascertain quantity, dimensions or capacity by any rule or standard.

METEYARD *n.*
A yard, staff or rod, used as a measure.

MIDDAY *n.*
The middle of the day; noon.

MIDST *n.*
The middle.

MIDWIFE *n.*
A woman that assists other women in childbirth.

MIGHT *n.*
1. Strength; force; power; primarily and chiefly, bodily strength or physical power.
2. Valor with bodily strength; military prowess.
3. Ability; strength or application of means.
4. Strength or force of purpose.
5. Strength of affection.

MILCH *a.*
Giving milk.

MILLET *n.*
A plant of the genus Milium.

MILLSTONE *n.*
A stone used for grinding grain.

MINCING *v.*
Cutting into small pieces; speaking or walking affectedly.

MIND *n.*
1. Intention; purpose; design.
2. Inclination; will; desire.
3. The intellectual or intelligent power in man; the understanding; the power that conceives, judges or reasons.
4. The heart or seat of affection.
5. The will and affection.
6. Opinion.
7. Memory; remembrance.
8. The implanted principle of grace.

MIND *v.*
To attend to; to fix the thoughts on; to regard with attention.

MINDFUL *a.*
Attentive; regarding with care; bearing in mind; heedful; observant.

MINGLE *v.*
1. To mix; to blend; to unite in one body.
2. To mix or blend without order or promiscuously.
3. To compound; to unite in a mass, as solid substances.
4. To join in mutual intercourse or in society.
5. To contaminate; to render impure; to debase by mixture.

MINISH *v.*
To lessen; to diminish.

MINISTER *n.*
1. Properly, a chief servant; an agent appointed to transact or manage business under the authority of another.
2. A magistrate; an executive officer.
3. A delegate; an embassador; the representative of a sovereign at a foreign court.
4. An angel; a messenger of God.

MINISTER *v.*
1. To attend and serve; to perform service in any office, sacred or secular.
2. To afford supplies; to give things needful; to supply the means of relief; to relieve.

MINISTRATION *n.*
1. The act of performing service as a subordinate agent; agency; intervention for aid or service.
2. Office of a minister; service; ecclesiastical function.

MINISTRY *n.*
The office, duties or functions of a subordinate agent of any kind.

MINSTREL *n.*
A singer and musical performer on instruments.

MIRE *n.*
Deep mud; earth so wet and soft as to yield to the feet and to wheels.

MIRTH *n.*
Social merriment; hilarity; high excitement of pleasurable feelings in company; noisy gayety; jollity.

MIRY *a.*
Abounding with deep mud; full of mire.

MISCARRYING *v.*
Failing of the intended effect; suffering abortion.

MISCHIEF *n.*
1. Harm; hurt; injury; damage; evil.
2. Ill consequence; evil; vexatious affair.

MISCHIEVOUS *a.*
Harmful; hurtful; injurious; making mischief.

MISTRESS *n.*
1. A woman who governs; correlative to servant, slave, or subject.
2. A female who is well skilled in any thing.

MITE *n.*
A small piece of money, the quarter of a denarius, or about seven English farthings.

MITRE *n.*
A sacerdotal ornament worn on the head by bishops and certain abbots, on solemn occasions.

MOCK *v.*
1. To imitate; to mimick; to imitate in contempt or derision; to mimick for the sake of derision; to deride by mimicry.
2. To deride; to laugh at; to ridicule; to treat with scorn or contempt.
3. To defeat; to illude; to disappoint; to deceive;
4. To fool; to tantalize; to play on in contempt.

MODERATION *n.*
1. Restraint of violent passions or indulgence of appetite.
2. Calmness of mind; equanimity.

MODEST *a.*
1. Properly, restrained by a sense of propriety; hence, not forward or bold; not presumptuous or arrogant; not boastful.
2. Not loose; not lewd.
3. Moderate; not excessive or extreme; not extravagant.

MOLLIFY *v.*
To soften; to make soft or tender.

MOLTEN *v.*

Made of melted metal.

MONEYCHANGER *n.*
A broker who deals in money or exchanges.

MONSTER *n.*
An animal produced with a shape or with parts that are not natural.

MONUMENT *n.*
1. Any thing by which the memory of a person or an event is preserved or per-petuated; a building, stone or other thing placed or erected to remind men of the person who raised it, or of a person deceased, or of any remarkable event.
2. A stone or a heap of stones or other durable thing, intended to mark the bounds of states, towns or distinct possessions, and preserve the memory of divisional lines.

MOREOVER *adv.*
Beyond what has been said; further; besides; also; likewise.

MORROW *n.*
1. The day next after the present.

2. The next day subsequent to any day specified.

MORTALITY *n.*
Subjection to death or the necessity of dying.

MORTALLY *adv.*
Irrecoverably; in a manner that must cause death; as mortally wounded.

MORTAR *n.*
A vessel of wood or metal in form of an inverted bell, in which substances are pounded or bruised with a pestle.

MORTGAGE *v.*
To grant an estate in fee as security for money lent or contracted to be paid at a certain time, on condition that if the debt shall be dis-charged according to the contract, the grant shall be void, otherwise to remain in full force.

MORTIFY *v.*
1. To destroy active pow-ers or essential qualities.
2. To subdue or bring into subjection.

MOTE *n.*

A small particle; any thing proverbially small; a spot.

MOURN *v.*
To express grief or sorrow; to grieve; to be sorrowful.

MOWER *n.*
One who mows; a man dexterous in the use of the scythe.

MOWN *a.*
Cleared of grass with a scythe.

MUFFLER *n.*
A cover for the face; a part of female dress.

MULTITUDE *n.*
1. The state of being many; a great number.
2. A number collectively; the sum of many.
3. A great number, indefinitely.
4. A crowd or throng; the populace.

MUNITION *n.*
Fortification.

MURMUR *v.*
1. To make a low continued noise.
2. To grumble; to com-

plain; to utter complaints in a low, half articulated voice; to utter sullen discontent.

MURRAIN *n.*
An infectious and fatal disease among cattle.

MUSE *v.*
To ponder; to think closely; to study in silence.

MUSE *v.*
To think on; to meditate on.

MUSTER *v.*
To collect troops for review, parade and exercise.

MUTTER *v.*
To utter with imperfect articulations, or with a low murmuring voice.

MUTUAL *a.*
Reciprocal; interchanged, each acting in return or correspondence to the other; given and received.

MUZZLE *v.*
To bind the mouth; to fasten the mouth to prevent biting or eating.

MYRRH *n.*
A gum-resin that comes in the form of drops or globules of various colors and sizes, of a pretty strong but agreeable smell, and of a bitter taste.

MYSTERY *n.*
1. A profound secret; something wholly unknown or something kept cautiously concealed, and therefore exciting curiosity or wonder.
2. Any thing in the character or attributes of God, or in the economy of divine providence, which is not revealed to man.
3. That which is beyond human comprehension until explained.

NAMELY *adv.*
To mention by name; particularly.

NARROW *a.*
1. Of little breadth; not wide or broad; having little distance from side to side.
2. Of little extent; very limited.

NAUGHT *n.*
Nothing.

NAUGHT *a.*
Bad; worthless; of no value or account.

NAUGHTINESS *a.*
Badness; wickedness; evil principle or purpose.

NAVEL *n.*
The center of the lower part of the abdomen, or the point where the umbilical cord passes out of the fetus.

NAY *adv.*
No; a word that expresses negation.

NECROMANCER *n.*
One who pretends to foretell future events by holding converse with departed spirits; a conjurer.

NEEDY *a.*
Necessitous; indigent; very poor; distressed by want of the means of living.

NEESING *n.*
A sneezing.

NEGLIGENT *a.*
Careless; heedless; apt or accustomed to omit what ought to be done; inatten-

tive to business or necessary concerns.

NEIGH *v.*
To utter the voice of a horse, expressive of want or desire; to whinny.

NEIGH *n.*
The voice of a horse; a whinnying.

NEIGHBOUR *n.*
1. One who lives near another.
2. One who lives in familiarity with another.
3. A fellow being.
4. One of the human race; any one that needs our help, or to whom we have an opportunity of doing good.

NETHER *a.*
Lower; lying or being beneath or in the lower part; opposed to upper.

NETHERMOST *a.*
Lowest.

NETTLE *n.*
A plant of the genus Urtica, whose prickles fret the skin and occasion very painful sensations.

NIGH *a.*
1. Near; not distant or remote in place or time.
2. Closely allied by blood.
3. Easy to be obtained or learnt; of easy access.
4. Ready to support, to forgive, or to aid and defend.
5. Close in fellowship; intimate in relation.
6. Near in progress or condition.

NITRE *n.*
A salt; stone-salt.

NOBLE *a.*
1. Great; elevated; dignified; being above every thing that can dishonor reputation.
2. Exalted; elevated; sublime.
3. Magnificent; stately; splendid.
4. Ingenuous; candid; of an excellent disposition; ready to receive truth.
5. Of the best kind; choice; excellent.

NOBLE *n.*
1. A person of honorable family or distinguished by station.
2. A person of rank above a commoner; a nobleman;

a peer.

NOISOME *a.*
1. Noxious to health; hurtful; mischievous; unwhole-
some; insalubrious; de-
structive.
2. Noxious; injurious.
3. Offensive to the smell
or other senses; disgusting;
fetid.

NOONIDE *n.*
The time of noon; mid-
day.

NOONTIDE *a.*
Pertaining to noon; merid-
ional.

NOTABLE *a.*
1. Remarkable; worthy of
notice; memorable; ob-
servable; distinguished or
noted.
2. Conspicuous; sightly.
3. Notorious.
4. Terrible.
5. Known or apparent.

NOUGHT *n.*
Nothing.

NOUGHT *a.*
Bad; worthless; of no
value or account.

NOURISH *v.*
1. To feed and cause to
grow; to supply a living or
organized body, animal or
vegetable, with matter
which increases its bulk or
supplies the waste occa-
sioned by any of its functions; to supply with nutri-
ment.
2. To support; to maintain
by feeding.
3. To cherish; to comfort.
4. To educate; to instruct;
to promote growth in at-
tainments.

NOVICE *n.*
One who is new in any
business; one unacquainted
or unskilled; one in the
rudiments; a beginner.

NURTURE *n.*
1. That which nourishes;
food; diet.
2. That which promotes
growth; education; instruction.

NURTURE *v.*
1. To feed; to nourish.
2. To educate; to bring or
train up.

OATH *n.*
A solemn affirmation or

declaration, made with an appeal to God for the truth of what is affirmed.

OBEDIENCE *n.*
Compliance with a command, prohibition or known law and rule of duty prescribed; the performance of what is required or enjoined by authority, or the abstaining from what is prohibited, in compliance with the command or prohibition.

OBEISANCE *n.*
A bow or courtesy; an act of reverence made by an inclination of the body or the knee.

OBEY *v.*
1. To comply with the commands, orders or instructions of a superior, or with the requirements of law, moral, political or municipal; to do that which is commanded or required, or to forbear doing that which is prohibited.
2. To submit to the government of; to be ruled by.
3. To submit to the direction or control of.
4. To yield to the impulse,

power or operation of.

OBLATION *n.*
Any thing offered or presented in worship or sacred service; an offering; a sacrifice.

OBSCURE *a.*
Dark; destitute of light.

OBSTINATE *a.*
Stubborn; pertinaciously adhering to an opinion or purpose; fixed firmly in resolution; not yielding to reason, arguments or other means.

OCCURRENT *n.*
Incident; any thing that happens.

ODIOUS *a.*
1. Hateful; deserving hatred.
2. Offensive to the senses; disgusting.

ODOUR *n.*
Smell; scent; fragrance; a sweet or an offensive smell; perfume.

OFFSCOURING *n.*
That which is scoured off; refuse; rejected matter; that

which is vile or despised.

OFFSPRING *n.*
1. A child or children; a descendant or descendants, however remote from the stock.
2. Propagation; generation.
3. Production of any kind.

OFT *adv.*
Often; frequently; not rarely.

OFTENTIMES *adv.*
Frequently; often; many times.

OINTMENT *n.*
Unguent; any soft, unctuous substance or compound, used for smearing.

OMER *n.*
A Hebrew measure containing ten baths, or seventy five gallons and five pints of liquids, and eight bushels of things dry; largest measure by the Jews.

OMITT *v.*
1. To leave, pass by or neglect; to fail or forbear to do or to use.
2. To leave out; not to insert or mention.

OMNIPOTENT *a.*
1. Almighty; possessing unlimited power; all powerful.
2. Having unlimited power of a particular kind.

ONWARD *a.*
Advanced or advancing.

OPPOSE *v.*
1. To set; against; to put in opposition, with a view to counterbalance or countervail; to hinder defeat, destroy or prevent effect.
2. To act against; to resist, either by physical means, by arguments or other means.
3. To check; to resist effectually.
4. To place in front; to set opposite.

OPPOSITION *n.*
1. Situation so as to front something else; a standing over against.
2. Resistance.

OPPRESS *v.*
1. To load or burden with unreasonable impositions; to treat with unjust severity, rigor or hardship.
2. To overpower; to over-

burden.

3. To sit or lie heavy on.

ORACLE *n.*

1. The communications, revelations or messages delivered by God to prophets.

2. The sanctuary or most holy place in the temple, in which was deposited the ark of the covenant.

ORATION *n.*

A speech or discourse composed according to the rules of oratory, and spoken in public.

ORATOR *n.*

A public speaker.

ORDAIN *v.*

1. Properly, to set; to establish in a particular office or order; to invest with a ministerial function or sacerdotal power.

2. To appoint; to decree.

3. To set; to establish; to institute; to constitute.

4. To set apart for an office; to appoint.

5. To appoint; to prepare.

ORDERLY *a.*

1. Methodical; regular.

2. Observant of order or method.

3. Well regulated; performed in good order; not tumultuous.

4. According to established method.

5. Not unruly; not inclined to break from inclosures; peaceable.

ORDINANCE *n.*

1. A rule established by authority; a permanent rule of action.

2. Observance commanded.

3. Appointment.

4. Established rite or ceremony.

ORNAMENT *n.*

1. That which embellishes; something which, added to another thing, renders it more beautiful to the eye.

2. The chains, and the bracelets, and the mufflers, the bonnets and the ornaments of the legs.

3. Embellishment; decoration; additional beauty.

ORPHAN *n.*

A child who is bereaved of father or mother or of both.

OSPRAY *n.*
The sea-eagle, a fowl of the genus Falco or hawk, of the size of a peacock.

OSSIFRAGE *n.*
The ospray or sea-eagle.

OUCHE *n.*
A bezil or socket in which a precious stone or seal is set.

OUGHT *v.*
1. To be held or bound in duty or moral obligation.
2. To be necessary.

OUTCAST *n.*
One who is cast out or expelled; an exile; one driven from home or country.

OUTLANDISH *a.*
Foreign; not native.

OUTRAGEOUS *a.*
1. Violent; furious; exorbitant; exceeding all bounds of moderation.
2. Excessive; exceeding reason or decency.

OUTWENT *past tense of outgo.*

OVERMUCH *a.*
Too much; exceeding what is necessary or proper.

OVERMUCH *adv.*
In too great a degree.

OVERMUCH *n.*
More than sufficient.

OVERSEE *v.*
To superintend; to overlook, implying care.

OVERSEER *n.*
One who overlooks; a superintendent; a supervisor.

OVERSHADOW *v.*
1. To throw a shadow over; to overshade.
2. To shelter; to protect; to cover with protecting influence.

OVERSIGHT *n.*
Superintendence; watchful care.

PACIFY *v.*
1. To appease; to calm; to still; to quiet; to allay agitation or excitement.
2. To restore peace to; to tranquilize.

PALMERWORM *n.*
A worm covered with hair.

PALSY *n.*
The loss or defect of the power of voluntary muscular motion in the whole body, or in a particular part; paralysis.

PANG *n.*
Extreme pain; anguish; agony of body; a sudden paroxysm of extreme pain.

PANT *v.*
1. To palpitate; to beat with preternatural violence or rapidity.
2. To long; to desire ardently.

PAP *n.*
A nipple of the breast; a teat.

PARABLE *n.*
A fable or allegorical relation or representation of something real in life or nature, from which a moral is drawn for instruction.

PARADISE *n.*
1. The garden of Eden, in which Adam and Eve were placed immediately after their creation.
2. A place of bliss; a region of supreme felicity or delight.
3. Heaven, the blissful seat of sanctified souls after death.

PARAMOUR *n.*
1. A lover; a wooer.
2. A mistress.

PARCEL *n.*
1. A part; a portion of any thing taken separately.
2. A quantity; any mass.

PARCHED *v.*
Scorched; dried to extremity.

PARCHMENT *n.*
The skin of a sheep or goat dressed or prepared and rendered fit for writing on.

PARDON *v.*
1. To forgive; to remit.
2. To remit.
3. To excuse.

PARDON *n.*
Forgiveness; the release of an offense or of the obligation of the offender to suffer a penalty, or to bear the displeasure of the offended party.

PARE *v.*

To cut off, as the superficial substance or extremities of a thing; to shave off with a sharp instrument.

PARLOUR *n.*
The room in a house which the family usually occupy when they have no company.

PARTIAL *a.*
1. Biased to one party; inclined to favor one party in a cause, or one side of a question, more than the other; not indifferent.
2. Inclined to favor without reason.
3. More strongly inclined to one thing than to others.

PASSION *n.*
The impression or effect of an external agent upon a body; that which is suffered or received.

PASSOVER *n.*
1. A feast of the Jews, instituted to commemorate the providential escape of the Hebrews, in Egypt, when God smiting the first -born of the Egyptians, passed over the houses of the Israelites, which were marked with the blood of the paschal lamb.
2. The sacrifice offered at the feast of the Passover.

PASTOR *n.*
1. A shepherd; one that has the care of flocks and herds.
2. A minister of the gospel who has the charge of a church and congregation, whose duty is to watch over the people of his charge, and instruct them in the sacred doctrines of the christian religion.

PATE *n.*
The head, or rather the top of the head.

PATIENCE *n.*
1. The suffering of afflictions, pain, toil, calamity, provocation or other evil, with a calm, unruffled temper; endurance without murmuring or fretfulness.
2. A calm temper which bears evils without murmuring or discontent.
3. The act or quality of waiting long for justice or expected good without discontent.
4. Perseverance; constancy

in labor or exertion.
5. The quality of bearing offenses and injuries without anger or revenge.

PAVILION *n.*
A tent; a temporary movable habitation.

PEACE *n.*
1. Freedom from agitation or disturbance by the passions, as from fear, terror, anger, anxiety or the like; quietness of mind; tranquillity; calmness; quiet of conscience.
2. Heavenly rest; the happiness of heaven.
3. Harmony; concord; a state of reconciliation between parties at variance.

PEACEMAKER *n.*
One who makes peace by reconciling parties that are at variance.

PECULIAR *a.*
1. Appropriate; belonging to a person and to him only.
2. Singular; particular.
3. Particular; special.

PEELED *v.*
Stripped of skin, bark or

rind; plundered; pillaged.

PEEP *v.*
To cry, as chickens; to utter a fine shrill sound.

PEN *n.*
An instrument used for writing, usually made of the quill of some large fowl.

PENTECOST *n.*
A solemn festival of the Jews, so called because celebrated on the fiftieth day after the sixteenth of Nisan, which was the second day of the passover.

PENURY *n.*
Want of property; indigence; extreme poverty.

PERADVENTURE *adv.*
By chance; perhaps; it may be.

PERDITION *n.*
1. Entire loss or ruin; utter destruction.
2. The utter loss of the soul or of final happiness in a future state; future misery or eternal death.

PERFECT *a.*

1. Finished; complete; consummate; not defective; having all that is requisite to its nature and kind.
2. Fully informed; completely skilled.
3. Complete in moral excellencies.
4. Manifesting perfection.

PERFECT *v.*
To finish or complete so as to leave nothing wanting; to give to any thing all that is requisite to its nature and kind.

PERIL *n.*
1. Danger; risk; hazard; jeopardy; particular exposure of person or property to injury, loss or destruction from any cause whatever.
2. Danger denounced; particular exposure.

PERISH *v.*
1. To die; to lose life in any manner; applied to animals.
2. To be destroyed; to come to nothing.
3. To fail entirely or to be extirpated.
4. To be burst or ruined.

5. To be wasted or rendered useless.
6. To be injured or tormented.
7. To be lost eternally; to be sentenced to endless misery.

PERNICIOUS *a.*
Destructive; having the quality of killing, destroying or injuring; very injurious or mischievous.

PERPLEXED *v.*
Made intricate; embarrassed; puzzled.

PERSECUTE *v.*
1. To pursue in a manner to injure, vex or afflict; to harass with unjust punishment or penalties for supposed offenses; to inflict pain from hatred or malignity.
2. To afflict, harass, or destroy for adherence to a particular creed or system of religious principles, or to a mode of worship.

PERSEVERANCE *n.*
1. Persistence in any thing undertaken; continued pursuit or prosecution of any business or enterprise be-

gun.

2. Continuance in a state of grace to a state of glory.

PERTAIN *v.*

1. To belong; to be the property, right or duty of.
2. To have relation to.

PERVERSE *a.*

1. Turned aside; distorted from the right.
2. Obstinate in the wrong; disposed to be contrary; stubborn; untractable.
3. Cross; petulant; peevish; disposed to cross and vex.

PERVERT *v.*

1. To turn from truth, propriety, or from its proper purpose; to distort from its true use or end.
2. To turn from the right; to corrupt.

PESTLE *n.*

An instrument for pounding and breaking substances in a mortar.

PETITION *n.*

A request, supplication or prayer; a solemn or formal supplication; a prayer addressed by a person to the Supreme Being, for some-thing needed or desired, or a branch or particular article of prayer.

PETITION *v.*

To make a request to; to ask from; to solicit; particularly, to make supplication to a superior for some favor or right.

PHARISEE *n.*

One of a sect among the Jews, whose religion consisted in a strict observance of rites and ceremonies and of the traditions of the elders, and whose pretended holiness led them to separate themselves as a sect, considering themselves as more righteous than other Jews.

PIETY *n.*

A compound of veneration or reverence of the Supreme Being and love of his character, or veneration accompanied with love; the exercise of these affections in obedience to his will and devotion to his service.

PILGRIM *n.*

1. A wanderer; a traveler.

2. One that has only a temporary residence on earth.

PILGRIMAGE *n.*
1. A long journey.
2. The journey of human life.

PILLED *a.* (1913)
Stripped of hair; scant of hair; bald.

PINE *v.*
To languish; to lose flesh or wear away under any distress of anxiety of mind; to grow lean.

PINNACLE *n.*
A high spiring point; summit.

PISS *v.*
To discharge the liquor secreted by the kidneys and lodged in the urinary bladder.

PISS *n.*
Urine; the liquor secreted by the kidneys into the bladder of an animal and discharged through the proper channel.

PITCH *n.*
1. A thick tenacious substance, the juice of a species of pine or fir called abies picea, obtained by incision from the bark of the tree.
2. The resin of pine, or turpentine, inspissated; used in caulking ships and paying the sides and bottom.

PITCH *v.*
1. To throw or thrust, and primarily, to thrust a long or pointed object; to fix; to plant; to set.
2. To fix a tent or temporary habitation; to encamp.

PLAGUE *n.*
1. Any thing troublesome or vexatious.
2. A pestilential disease.
3. A state of misery.
4. Any great natural evil or calamity.

PLAGUE *v.*
To infest with disease, calamity or natural evil of any kind.

PLAISTER *n.*
A composition of lime, water and sand, well mixed into a kind of paste and used for coating walls and partitions of houses.

PLASTER *v.*
To cover with plaster.

PLAITING *v.*
Folding; doubling; braiding.

PLANE *n.*
A scraper; a carving chisel.

PLAT *v.*
To weave; to form by texture.

PLEA *n.*
A cause in court; a lawsuit, or a criminal process.

PLEASE *v.*
1. To excite agreeable sensations or emotions in; to gratify.
2. To satisfy; to content.

PLEASURE *n.*
1. The gratification of the senses or of the mind; agreeable sensations or emotions; the excitement, relish or happiness produced by enjoyment or the expectation of good; opposed to pain.
2. What the will dictates or prefers; will; choice; purpose; intention; command.

PLEDGE *n.*
1. Something put in pawn; that which is deposited with another as security for the repayment of money borrowed, or for the performance of some agreement or obligation; a pawn.
2. Any thing given or considered as a security for the performance of an act.

PLOT *v.*
To make a plan of; to delineate.

PLOT *n.*
Any scheme, stratagem or plan of a complicated nature, or consisting of many parts, adapted to the accomplishment of some purpose.

PLOWSHARE *n.*
The part of a plow which cuts the ground at the bottom of the furrow, and raises the slice to the mould-board, which turns it over.

PLUCK *v.*
1. To pull with sudden force or effort, or to pull off, out or from, with a

twitch.
2. To strip by plucking.

POLL *v.*
To clip; to cut off the ends; to cut off hair or wool; to shear.

POLLUTED *v.*
Defiled; rendered unclean; tainted with guilt; impaired; profaned.

POMMEL *n.*
A knob or ball.

POMP *n.*
1. A procession distinguished by ostentation of grandeur and splendor.
2. Show of magnificence; parade; splendor.

PONDER *v.*
1. To weigh in the mind; to consider and compare the circumstances or consequences of an event, or the importance of the reasons for or against a decision.
2. To view with deliberation; to examine.

PORT *n.*
A harbor; a haven; any bay, cove, inlet or recess of the sea or of a lake or the mouth of a river, which ships or vessels can enter, and where they can lie safe from injury by storms.

PORTER *n.*
A man that has the charge of a door or gate; a door-keeper.

POTENTATE *n.*
A person who possesses great power or sway; a prince; a sovereign; an emperor, king or monarch.

POTSHERD *n.*
A piece or fragment of a broken pot.

POTTAGE *n.*
Broth; soup.

POURTRAY *v.*
To paint or draw the likeness of any thing in colors.

POWER *n.*
1. The faculty of doing or performing any thing; the faculty of moving or of producing a change in something; ability or strength.
2. Force; strength; energy.
3. Ability, natural or

moral.

4. Force; strength; momentum.

5. Command; the right of governing, or actual government; dominion; rule, sway; authority.

6. One invested with authority; a ruler; a civil magistrate.

7. Legal authority.

8. Right; privilege.

PRAISE *v.*

1. To commend; to applaud; to express approbation of personal worth or actions.

2. To extol in words or song; to magnify; to glorify on account of perfections or excellent.

3. To express gratitude for personal favors.

4. To do honor to; to display the excellence of.

PRATING *n.*

Talking much on a trifling subject; talking idly.

PRAYER *n.*

1. The act of asking for a favor, and particularly with earnestness.

2. A solemn address to the Supreme Being, consisting of adoration, or an expression of our sense of God's glorious perfections, confession of our sins, supplication for mercy and forgiveness, intercession for blessings on others, and thanksgiving, or an expression of gratitude to God for his mercies and benefits.

PREACH *v.*

1. To pronounce a public discourse on a religious subject, or from a subject, or from a text of Scripture.

2. To discourse on the gospel way of salvation and exhort to repentance; to discourse on evangelical truths and exhort to a belief of them and acceptance of the terms of salvation.

PREACH *v.*

To proclaim; to publish in religious discourses.

PREACH *n.*

A religious discourse.

PRECEPT *n.*

1. Any commandment or order intended as an authoritative rule of action.

2. A command or mandate in writing.

PRECIOUS *a.*
1. Of great price; costly.
2. Of great value or worth; very valuable.
3. Highly valued; much esteemed.

PREDESTINATE *v.*
To predetermine or foreordain; to appoint or ordain beforehand by an unchangeable purpose.

PREDESTINATED *v.*
Predetermined; foreordained; decreed.

PREEMINENCE *n.*
1. Superiority in excellence; distinction in something commendable.
2. Precedence; priority of place; superiority in rank or dignity.

PRESBYTERY *n.*
A body of elders in the Christian church.

PRESERVE *v.*
1. To keep or save from injury or destruction; to defend from evil.
2. To uphold; to sustain.

3. To save from decay; to keep in a sound state.
4. To keep or defend from corruption.

PRESSFAT *n.*
A trough; a wine vat.

PRESUMPTUOUS *a.*
1. Willful; done with bold design, rash confidence or in violation of known duty.
2. Bold and confident to excess; adventuring without reasonable ground of success; hazarding safety on too slight grounds; rash.
3. Founded on presumption; proceeding from excess of confidence.
4. Unduly confident; irreverent with respect to sacred things.

PRETENCE *n.*
A holding out or offering to others something false or feigned; a presenting to others, either in words or actions, a false or hypocritical appearance.

PREVAIL *v.*
To overcome; to gain the victory or superiority; to gain the advantage.

PREVENT *v.*
To go before; to precede.

PRAY *v.*
1. To ask with earnestness or zeal; to entreat; to supplicate.
2. To petition; to ask.
3. To address the Supreme Being with solemnity and reverence, with adoration, confession of sins, supplication for mercy, and thanksgiving for blessings received.

PRICK *n.*
A slender pointed instrument or substance, which is hard enough to pierce the skin; a goad; a spur.

PRIDE *n.*
1. Inordinate self-esteem; an unreasonable conceit of one's own superiority in talents, beauty, wealth, accomplishments, rank or elevation in office, which manifests itself in lofty airs, distance, reserve, and often in contempt of others.
2. Insolence; rude treatment of others; insolent exultation.
3. Elevation; loftiness.

PRIEST *n.*
A man who officiates in sacred offices.

PRINCIPAL *a.*
1. Chief; highest in rank, character or respectability.
2. Chief; most important or considerable.

PRINCIPALITY *n.*
1. Sovereignty; supreme power.
2. A prince; one invested with sovereignty.
3. Royal state or attire.

PRIVILY *adv.*
Privately; secretly.

PRIVY *a.*
1. Private; pertaining to some person exclusively; assigned to private uses; not public.
2. Appropriated to retirement; not shown; not open for the admission of company.
3. Privately knowing; admitted to the participation of knowledge with another of a secret transaction.

PROCLAIM *v.*
1. To promulgate; to announce; to publish.

2. To utter openly; to make public.

PROCURE *v.*
To get; to gain; to obtain.

PROFANE *a.*
1. Irreverent to any thing sacred.
2. Not purified or holy; allowed for common use.
3. Obscene; heathenish; tending to bring reproach on religion.

PROFANE *v.*
1. To violate any thing sacred, or treat it with abuse, irreverence, obloquy or contempt.
2. To pollute; to defile.
3. To violate.
4. To pollute; to debase.

PROFESS *v.*
1. To make open declaration of; to avow or acknowledge.
2. To declare in strong terms.

PROFOUND *a.*
Deep in skill or contrivance.

PROGENITOR *n.*
An ancestor in the direct line; a forefather.

PROGNOSTICATOR *n.*
A foreknower or foreteller of a future event by present signs.

PROLONG *v.*
1. To lengthen in time; to extend the duration of.
2. To lengthen; to draw out in time by delay; to continue.
3. To put off to a distant time.
4. To extend in space or length.

PROMISE *n.*
1. In a general sense, a declaration, written or verbal, made by one person to another, which binds the person who makes it, either in honor, conscience or law, to do or forbear a certain act specified; a declaration which gives to the person to whom it is made, a right to expect or to claim the performance or forbearance of the act.
2. A binding declaration of something to be done or given for another's benefit.
3. That which is promised; fulfillment or grant of what

is promised.

PROMISE *v.*
1. To make a declaration to another, which binds the promiser in honor, conscience or law, to do or forbear some act.
2. To afford reason to expect.
3. To make declaration or give assurance of some benefit to be conferred; to pledge or engage to bestow.

PROPHECY *n.*
1. A foretelling; prediction; a declaration of something to come.
2. A book of prophecies; a history.
3. Preaching; public interpretation of Scripture; exhortation or instruction.

PROPHESY *v.*
1. To utter predictions; to make declaration of events to come.
2. To preach; to instruct in religious doctrines; to interpret or explain Scripture or religious subjects; to exhort.

PROPHET *n.*

1. One that foretells future events; a predicter; a foreteller.
2. A person illuminated, inspired or instructed by God to announce future events.
3. An interpreter; one that explains or communicates sentiments.

PROPITIATION *n.*
1. The act of appeasing wrath and conciliating the favor of an offended person; the act of making propitious.
2. The atonement or atoning sacrifice offered to God to assuage his wrath and render him propitious to sinners.

PROSELYTE *n.*
A new convert to some religion or religious sect, or to some particular opinion, system or party.

PROSPECT *n.*
Position of the front of a building; as a prospect towards the south or north.

PROUD *a.*
1. Having inordinate self-esteem; possessing a high

or unreasonable conceit of one's own excellence, either of body or mind.
2. Arrogant; haughty; supercilious.
3. Daring; presumptuous.

PROVENDER *n.*
Dry food for beasts, usually meal, or a mixture of meal and cut straw or hay.

PROVERB *n.*
1. A short sentence often repeated, expressing a well known truth or common fact, ascertained by experience or observation; a maxim of wisdom.
2. A moral sentence or maxim that is enigmatical; a dark saying of the wise that requires interpretation.
3. A by-word; a name often repeated; a reproach or object of contempt.

PROVIDENCE *n.*
1. Foresight; timely care; particularly, active foresight, or foresight accompanied with the procurement of what is necessary for future use, or with suitable preparation.
2. The care and superintendence which God exercises over his creatures.

PROVOKE *v.*
1. To call into action; to arouse; to excite.
2. To make angry; to offend; to incense; to enrage.
3. To excite; to cause.
4. To move; to incite; to stir up; to induce by motives.

PRUDENCE *n.*
Wisdom applied to practice.

PRUDENT *a.*
Cautious; circumspect; practically wise; careful of the consequences of enterprises, measures or actions; cautious not to act when the end is of doubtful utility, or probably impracticable.

PSALM *n.*
A sacred song or hymn; a song composed on a divine subject and in praise of God.

PSALTERY *n.*
An instrument of music used by the Hebrews, the form of which is not now known.

PUBLICAN *n.*
A collector of toll or tribute.

PULSE *n.*
Leguminous plants or their seeds.

PUNISHMENT *n.*
Any pain or suffering inflicted on a person for a crime or offense, by the authority to which the offender is subject, either by the constitution of God or of civil society.

PURE *a.*
1. Unmixed; separate from any other subject or from every thing foreign.
2. Free from moral defilement; without spot; not sullied or tarnished; incorrupt; undebased by moral turpitude; holy.
3. Genuine; real; true; incorrupt; unadulterated.
4. Free from guilt; guiltless; innocent.
5. Free from vice or moral turpitude.
6. Ceremonially clean; unpolluted.

PURGE *v.*
1. To cleanse or purify by separating and carrying off whatever is impure, heterogeneous, foreign or superfluous.
2. To clear from guilt or moral defilement; to purge away sin.
3. To remove what is offensive; to sweep away impurities.

PURIFICATION *n.*
1. The act of purifying; the act or operation of separating and removing from any thing that which is heterogeneous or foreign to it.
2. The act or operation of cleansing ceremonially, by removing any pollution or defilement.
3. A cleansing from guilt or the pollution of sin; the extinction of sinful desires, appetites and inclinations.

PURIFY *v.*
1. To make pure or clear; to free from extraneous admixture.
2. To free from pollution ceremonially; to remove whatever renders unclean and unfit for sacred services.
3. To free from guilt or the defilement of sin.

PURITY *n.*
1. Freedom from foreign admixture or heterogeneous matter.
2. Cleanness; freedom from foulness or dirt.
3. Freedom from guilt or the defilement of sin.
4. Chastity; freedom from contamination by illicit sexual connection.

PURLOIN *v.*
Literally, to take or carry away for one's self; to steal; to take by theft.

PURPOSE *v.*
To intend; to design; to resolve; to determine on some end or object to be accomplished.

PURTENANCE *n.*
That which belongs to something else; an appendage.

PUTRIFY *v.*
1. To corrupt; to make foul.
2. To make morbid, carious or gangrenous.

QUAIL *n.*
A bird of the genus Tetrao or grouse kind.

QUARRY *n.*
1. A place, cavern or pit where stones are dug from the earth, or separated from a large mass of rocks.
2. A square.

QUENCH *v.*
1. To extinguish; to put out.
2. To still; to quiet; to repress.
3. To destroy.
4. To check; to stifle.

QUICK *v.*
To stir; to move.

QUICK *a.*
Alive; living; opposed to dead or unanimated.

QUICKEN *v.*
1. Primarily, to make alive; to vivify; to revive or resuscitate.
2. To make alive in a spiritual sense; to communicate a principle of grace to.
3. To revive; to cheer; to reinvigorate; to refresh by new supplies of comfort or grace.

QUIT *v.*
1. To free; to clear; to liberate; to discharge from.

2. To carry through; to do or perform something to the end, so that nothing remains; to discharge or perform completely.
3. To quit one's self, reciprocally, to clear one's self of incumbent duties by full performance.

QUIVER *n.*
A case or sheath for arrows.

RABBI *n.*
A title assumed by the Jewish doctors, signifying master or lord.

RACA *n.*
A Syriac word signifying empty, beggarly, foolish; a term of extreme contempt.

RAIL *v.*
To utter reproaches; to scoff; to use insolent and reproachful language; to reproach or censure in opprobrious terms.

RAIMENT *n.*
Clothing in general; vestments; vesture; garments.

RAMPART *n.*
That which fortifies and defends from assault; that which secures safety.

RANGING *v.*
Roving; passing near and in the direction of.

RANK *past tense of ring.*

RAVENING *v.*
Preying with rapacity; voraciously devouring.

RAVENING *n.*
Eagerness for plunder.

RAVISH *v.*
1. To seize and carry away by violence.
2. To have carnal knowledge of a woman by force and against her consent.
3. To bear away with joy or delight; to delight to ecstasy; to transport.

REAP *v.*
1. To cut grain with a sickle.
2. To gather; to obtain; to receive as a reward, or as the fruit of labor or of works.

REBEL *n.*
1. One who revolts from the government to which

he owes allegiance.
2. One who willfully violates a law.
3. One who disobeys the king's proclamation; a contemner of the king's laws.
4. A villain who disobeys his lord.

REBELLION *n.*

1. An open and avowed renunciation of the authority of the government to which one owes allegiance.
2. Open resistance to lawful authority.

REBUKE *v.*

1. To chide; to reprove; to reprehend for a fault; to check by reproof.
2. To chasten; to punish; to afflict for correction.
3. To check; to silence.
4. To check; to heal.
5. To restrain; to calm.

REBUKE *n.*

1. Chastisement; punishment; affliction for the purpose of restraint and correction.
2. A chiding; reproof for faults; reprehension.
3. Any kind of check.

RECOMPENCE *v.*

1. To compensate; to make return of an equivalent for any thing given, done or suffered.
2. To requite; to repay; to return an equivalent.
3. To make restitution or an equivalent return for.

RECONCILE *v.*

1. To conciliate anew; to call back into union and friendship the affections which have been alienated; to restore to friendship or favor after estrangement.
2. To bring to acquiescence, content or quiet submission; with to.

RECONCILIATION *n.*

1. The act of reconciling parties at variance; renewal of friendship after disagreement or enmity.
2. The means by which sinners are reconciled and brought into a state of favor with God, after natural estrangement or enmity; the atonement; expiation.
3. Agreement of things seemingly opposite, different or inconsistent.

REDEEMED *v.*

Ransomed; delivered from bondage, distress, penalty, liability, or from the possession of another, by paying an equivalent.

REDEMPTION *n.*
1. Repurchase of captured goods or prisoners; the act of procuring the deliverance of persons or things from the possession and power of captors by the payment of an equivalent; ransom; release.
2. The purchase of God's favor by the death and sufferings of Christ; the ransom or deliverance of sinners from the bondage of sin and the penalties of God's violated law by the atonement of Christ.
3. Deliverance from bondage, distress, or from liability to any evil or forfeiture, either by money, labor or other means.

REDOUND *v.*
1. To be sent, rolled or driven back.
2. To conduce in the consequence; to contribute; to result.

REFORM *v.*

1. To change from worse to better; to amend; to correct; to restore to a former good state, or to bring from a bad to a good state.
2. To change from bad to good; to remove that which is bad or corrupt.

REFORM *v.*
To abandon that which is evil or corrupt, and return to a good state; to be amended or corrected.

REFRAIN *v.*
1. To hold back; to restrain; to keep from action.
2. To forbear; to abstain.

REFUGE *n.*
1. Shelter or protection from danger or distress.
2. That which shelters or protects from danger, distress or calamity; a strong hold which protects by its strength, or a sanctuary which secures safety by its sacredness; any place inaccessible to an enemy.

REFUSE *n.*
That which is refused or rejected as useless; waste matter.

REIGN *v.*
1. To possess or exercise sovereign power or authority; to rule; to exercise government; or to hold the supreme power.
2. To be predominant; to prevail.
3. To rule; to have superior or uncontrolled dominion.

REINS *n.*
1. The kidneys; the lower part of the back.
2. The inward parts; the heart, or seat of the affections and passions.

RELIGION *n.*
1. A belief in the being and perfections of God, in the revelation of his will to man, in man's obligation to obey his commands, in a state of reward and punishment, and in man's accountableness to God; true godliness or piety of life, with the practice of all moral duties.
2. Godliness or real piety in practice, consisting in the performance of all known duties to God and our fellow men, in obedience to divine command, or from love to God and his law.
3. The performance of the duties we owe directly to God, from a principle of obedience to his will.

REMISSION *n.*
1. Release; discharge or relinquishment of a claim or right.
2. Forgiveness; pardon; the giving up of the punishment due to a crime.

REMIT *v.*
1. To relax, as intensity; to make less tense or violent.
2. To forgive; to surrender the right of punishing a crime.
3. To pardon, as a fault or crime.

REMNANT *n.*
Residue; that which is left after the separation, removal or destruction of a part.

REND *v.*
1. To separate any substance into parts with force or sudden violence; to tear asunder; to split.
2. To separate or part with violence.

RENOUNCE *v.*

1. To disown; to disclaim; to reject; to refuse to own or acknowledge as belonging to.
2. To deny; to cast off; to reject; to disclaim.
3. To cast off or reject; to forsake.

RENOWN *n.*

Fame; celebrity; exalted reputation derived from the extensive praise of great achievements or accomplishments.

RENT *v.*

Torn asunder; split or burst by violence; torn.

RENT *v.*

To tear.

REPENT *v.*

1. To change the mind.
2. To sorrow or be pained for sin, as a violation of God's holy law, a dishonor to his character and government, and the foulest ingratitude to a Being of infinite benevolence.
3. To feel pain, sorrow or regret for something done or spoken.

REPENTANCE *n.*

1. A change of mind; a conversion from sin to God.
2. Real penitence; sorrow or deep contrition for sin, as an offense and dishonor to God, a violation of his holy law, and the basest ingratitude towards a Being of infinite benevolence.
3. Sorrow for any thing done or said; the pain, regret or affliction which a person feels on account of his past conduct.

REPLENISH *v.*

To fill; to stock with numbers or abundance.

REPROACH *v.*

1. To censure in terms of opprobrium or contempt.
2. To charge with a fault in severe language.
3. To upbraid; to suggest blame for any thing.
4. To treat with scorn or contempt.

REPROACH *n.*

1. Censure mingled with contempt or derision; contumelious or opprobrious language towards any per-

son; abusive reflections.
2. Shame; infamy; dis-
grace.
3. Object of contempt,
scorn or derision.
4. That which is the cause
of shame or disgrace.

REPROBATE *a.*
1. Not enduring proof or
trial; not of standard purity
or fineness; disallowed;
rejected.
2. Abandoned in sin; lost
to virtue or grace.
3. Abandoned to error, or
in apostasy.

REPROOF *n.*
1. Blame expressed to the
face; censure for a fault;
reprehension.
2. Blame cast; censure directed to a person.

REPROVE *v.*
1. To blame; to censure.
2. To charge with a fault to
the face; to chide; to reprehend.
3. To convince of a fault,
or to make it manifest.
4. To excite a sense of
guilt.

REPUTE *v.*
To think; to account; to

hold; to reckon.

REPUTE *n.*
1. Reputation; good char-
acter; the credit or honor
derived from common or
public opinion.
2. Character.
3. Established opinion.

REQUITE *v.*
1. To repay either good or
evil; in a good sense, to
recompense; to return an
equivalent in good; to reward.
2. To do or give in return.

REREWARD *n.*
The part of an army that
marches in the rear; the
rear guard.

RESPITE *n.*
Pause; temporary intermission of labor, or of any
process or operation; inter-
val of rest.

RESURRECTION *n.*
A rising again; the revival
of the dead of the human
race, or their return from
the grave.

REVEAL *v.*
1. To disclose; to discover;

to show; to make known something before unknown or concealed.
2. To disclose, discover or make known from heaven.

REVEL *v.*
1. To feast with loose and clamorous merriment; to carouse.
2. To move playfully or without regularity.

REVENGE *v.*
To vindicate by punishment of an enemy.

REVENGE *n.*
1. Return of an injury; the deliberate infliction of pain or injury or a person in return for an injury received from him.
2. The passion which is excited by an injury done or an affront given; the desire of inflicting pain on one who has done an injury.

REVENUE *n.*
1. Return; reward.
2. The annual produce of taxes, excise, customs, duties, rents, &c. which a nation or state collects and receives into the treasury

for public use.

REVERENCE *n.*
1. Fear mingled with respect and esteem; veneration.
2. An act of respect or obeisance.

REVERENCE *v.*
To regard with reverence; to regard with fear mingled with respect and affection.

REVEREND *a.*
Worthy of reverence; entitled to respect mingled with fear and affection.

REVILE *v.*
To reproach; to treat with opprobrious and contemptuous language.

REVOLT *v.*
1. To reject the authority of a sovereign.
2. To disclaim allegiance and subjection to God; to reject the government of the King of kings.

REWARD *v.*
To give in return, either good or evil.

REWARD *n.*

1. Recompense, or equivalent return for good done, for kindness, for services and the like.
2. The fruit of men's labor or works.
3. Punishment; a just return of evil or suffering for wickedness.

RIBBAND *n.*
A fillet of silk; a narrow web of silk used for an ornament.

RICH *a.*
1. Wealthy; opulent; possessing a large portion of land, goods or money, or a larger portion than is common to other men or to men of like rank.
2. Splendid; costly; valuable; precious; sumptuous.

RIDDANCE *n.*
1. Deliverance; a setting free.
2. The act of clearing away.

RIE *n.*
An esculent grain of the genus Secale, of a quality inferior to wheat, constituting a large portion of bread stuff.

RIFLE *v.*
1. To seize and bear away by force; to snatch away.
2. To strip; to rob; to pillage; to plunder.

RIGHTEOUS *a.*
1. Just; accordant to the divine law.
2. One who is holy in heart, and observant of the divine commands in practice.
3. Consonant to the divine will or to justice.
4. Just; equitable; merited.

RIGHTEOUSNESS *n.*
1. Purity of heart and rectitude of life; conformity of heart and life to the divine law.
2. The perfection or holiness of God's nature; exact rectitude; faithfulness.
3. The active and passive obedience of Christ, by which the law of God is fulfilled.
4. Justice; equity between man and man.

RIGOUR *n.*
1. Severity of life; austerity; voluntary submission to pain, abstinence or mortification.

2. Strictness; exactness without allowance, latitude or indulgence.

RINGSTRAKED *n.*
Having circular streaks or lines on the body.

RIOT *n.*
  1. Tumult; uproar.
  2. Wild and noisy festivity.
  3. Luxury.

RIOT *v.*
  1. To revel; to run to excess in feasting, drinking or other sensual indulgences.
  2. To luxuriate; to be highly excited.
  3. To raise an uproar or sedition.

RITE *n.*
The manner of performing divine or solemn service as established by law, precept or custom; formal act of religion, or other solemn duty.

ROEBUCK *n.*
  1. A species of deer, the Cervus capreolus, with erect cylindrical branched horns, forked at the summit.

2. Roe, the female of the hart.

ROLLER *n.*
A bandage; a fillet; a long broad bandage used in surgery.

ROUSE *v.*
  1. To awake from sleep or repose.
  2. To be excited to thought or action from a state of indolence, sluggishness, languor or inattention.

ROVER *n.*
A robber or pirate; a freebooter.

RUBBISH *n.*
  1. Fragments of buildings; broken or imperfect pieces of any structure; ruins.
  2. Waste or rejected matter; any thing worthless.

RUDE *a.*
  1. Rough; uneven; rugged; unformed by art.
  2. Raw; untaught; ignorant; not skilled or practiced.
  3. Artless; inelegant; not polished.

RUDIMENT *n.*

A first principle or element; that which is to be first learnt.

RUE *n.*
A plant of the genus Ruta, of several species.

RUINOUS *a.*
1. Fallen to ruin; entirely decayed; demolished; dilapidated.
2. Composed of ruins; consisting in ruins.

RUMP *n.*
The end of the back bone of an animal with the parts adjacent.

RUSH *n.*
A plant of the genus Juncus of many species.

SABAOTH *n.*
Armies.

SABBATH *n.*
1. The day which God appointed to be observed by the Jews as a day of rest from all secular labor or employments, and to be kept holy and consecrated to his service and worship.
2. Intermission of pain or sorrow; time of rest.

3. The sabbatical year among the Israelites.

SACKBUT *n.*
A wind instrument of music; a kind of trumpet, so contrived that it can be lengthened or shortened according to the tone required.

SACRIFICE *v.*
1. To offer to God in homage or worship, by killing and consuming; to immolate, either as an atonement for sin, or to procure favor, or to express thankfulness.
2. To destroy, surrender or suffer to be lost for the sake of obtaining something.
3. To destroy; to kill.

SACRIFICE *n.*
1. An offering made to God by killing and burning some animal upon an altar, as an acknowledgment of his power and providence, or to make atonement for sin, appease his wrath or conciliate his favor, or to express thankfulness for his benefits.
2. The thing offered to God, or immolated by an

act of religion.

3. Destruction, surrender or loss made or incurred for gaining some object, or for obliging another.

4. Any thing destroyed.

SACRILEGE *n.*
The crime of violating or profaning sacred things.

SADDUCEES *n.*
A sect among the jews who denied the resurrection, a future state, and the existence of angels.

SAFFRON *n.*
A plant of the genus Crocus.

SAINT *n.*
1. A person sanctified; a holy or godly person; one eminent for piety and virtue.
2. One of the blessed in heaven.

SAITH *present tense of say.*

SALUTATION *n.*
The act of saluting; a greeting; the act of paying respect or reverence by the customary words or actions; as in inquiring of persons their welfare, expressing to them kind wishes, bowing, &c.

SALUTE *v.*
1. To greet; to hail; to address with expressions of kind wishes.
2. To please; to gratify.
3. To kiss.

SALUTE *n.*
1. The act of expressing kind wishes or respect; salutation; greeting.
2. A kiss.

SALVATION *n.*
1. The act of saving; preservation from destruction, danger or great calamity.
2. The redemption of man from the bondage of sin and liability to eternal death, and the conferring on him everlasting happiness.
3. Deliverance from enemies; victory.
4. Remission of sins, or saving graces.
5. The author of man's salvation.

SANCTIFICATION *n.*
1. The act of making holy.

2. The act of God's grace by which the affections of men are purified or alienated from sin and the world, and exalted to a supreme love to God.
3. The act of consecrating or of setting apart for a sacred purpose; consecration.

SANCTIFIED *v.*
1. Made holy; consecrated; set apart for sacred services.
2. Affectedly holy.

SANCTIFY *v.*
1. In a general sense, to cleanse, purify or make holy.
2. To cleanse from corruption; to purify from sin; to make holy be detaching the affections from the world and its defilements, and exalting them to a supreme love to God.
3. To separate, set apart or appoint to a holy, sacred or religious use.
4. To purify; to prepare for divine service, and for partaking of holy things.
5. To secure from violation.

SANCTUARY *n.*
1. A sacred place; the most retired part of the temple at Jerusalem, called the Holy of Holies
2. The temple at Jerusalem.
3. A place of protection; a sacred asylum.
4. Shelter; protection.

SATAN *n.*
The grand adversary of man; the devil or prince of darkness; the chief of the fallen angels.

SATIATE *v.*
1. To fill; to satisfy appetite or desire; to feed to the full, or to furnish enjoyment to the extent of desire.
2. To fill to the extent of want.
3. To glut; to fill beyond natural desire.

SATYR *n.*
A monster, half man and half goat, having horns on his head, a hairy body, with the feet and tail of a goat.

SAVE *v.*
1. To preserve from injury,

destruction or evil of any kind; to rescue from danger.

2. To preserve from final and everlasting destruction; to rescue from eternal death.

3. To deliver; to rescue from the power and pollution of sin.

4. To except; to reserve from a general admission or account.

SAVED *v.*
Preserved from evil; injury or destruction; kept frugally; prevented; spared; taken in time.

SAVIOUR *n.*
1. Jesus Christ, the Redeemer, who has opened the way to everlasting salvation by his obedience and death.

2. One that saves or preserves.

SAVOUR *n.*
1. Taste or odor; something that perceptibly affects the organs of taste and smell.

2. The quality which renders a thing valuable; the quality which renders

other bodies agreeable to the taste.

SAVOURY *a.*
Pleasing to the organs of smell or taste.

SCABBARD *n.*
The sheath of a sword.

SCABBARD *v.*
To put in a sheath.

SCALL *n.*
Scab; scabbiness; leprosy.

SCANT *v.*
1. To limit; to straiten.
2. To fail or become less.

SCANT *a.*
Not full, large or plentiful; scarcely sufficient; rather less than is wanted for the purpose.

SCAPEGOAT *n.*
A goat which was brought to the door of the tabernacle, where the high priest laid his hands upon him, confessing the sins of the people, and putting them on the head of the goat.

SCARCE *a.*
1. Not plentiful or abun-

dant; being in small quantity in proportion to the demand.

2. Being few in number and scattered; rare; uncommon.

SCATTER *v.*

1. To disperse; to dissipate; to separate or remove things to a distance from each other.

2. To throw loosely about; to sprinkle.

3. To spread or set thinly.

SCEPTRE *n.*

1. A staff or batton borne by kings on solemn occasions, as a badge of authority.

2. Royal power or authority.

SCHISM *n.*

1. Division or separation.

2. A division or separation in a church occasioned by diversity of opinions; breach of unity among people of the same religious faith.

3. A breach of charity, rather than a difference of doctrine.

4. Separation; division among tribes or classes of people.

SCOFF *v.*

1. Ridicule, mockery or contumelious language; to manifest contempt by derision; with at.

2. To treat with derision or scorn.

SCORN *n.*

1. Extreme contempt; that disdain which springs from a person's opinion of the meanness of an object, and a consciousness or belief of his own superiority or worth.

2. A subject of extreme contempt, disdain or derision; that which is treated with contempt.

SCORN *v.*

1. To hold in extreme contempt; to despise; to contemn; to disdain.

2. To think unworth; to disdain.

3. To slight; to disregard; to neglect.

SCOUR *v.*

1. To rub hard with something rough, for the purpose of cleaning.

2. To clean by friction; to

make clean or bright.

SCOURGE *n.*

1. To whip; a lash consisting of a strap or cord; an instrument of punishment or discipline.
2. A punishment; vindictive affliction.
3. A whip for a top.

SCOURGE *v.*

1. To whip severely; to lash.
2. To punish with severity; to chastise; to afflict for sins or faults, and with the purpose of correction.
3. To afflict greatly; to harass, torment or injure.

SCRABBLE *v.*

To make irregular or crooked marks.

SCRIBE *n.*

1. A writer and a doctor of the law; a man of learning; one skilled in the law; one who read and explained the law to the people.
2. A clerk or secretary to the king.
3. An officer who enrolled or kept the rolls of the army, and called over the names and reviewed them.

SCRIBE *v.*

To mark by a model or rule; to mark so as to fit one piece to another; a term used by carpenters and joiners.

SCRIP *n.*

A small bag; a wallet; a satchel.

SCRIPTURE *n.*

1. The sacred writings or divine oracles, called sacred or holy, as proceeding from God and containing sacred doctrines and precepts.
2. The books of the Old and New Testament; the Bible.

SCUM *n.*

1. The extraneous matter or impurities which rise to the surface of liquors in boiling or fermentation, or which form on the surface by other means.
2. The refuse; the recrement; that which is vile or worthless.

SCURVY *n.*

A disease characterized by great debility, a pale bloated face, bleeding spongy gums, large livid tumors on the body, offensive breath, aversion to exercise, oppression at the breast or difficult respiration, a smooth, dry, shining skin, &c.

SEA *n.*
1. A large bason, cisternor laver which Solomon made in the temple, so large as to contain more than six thousand gallons.
2. A large body of water, nearly inclosed by land.

SEARED *v.*
Burnt on the surface; cauterized; hardened.

SEATWARD *n.* (Strongs)
Lid; Cover of the sacred ark.

SECT *n.*
A body or number of persons united in tenets, but constituting a distinct party by holding sentiments different from those of other men.

SEDITION *n.*
A factious commotion of the people, a tumultuous assembly of men rising in opposition to law or the administration of justice, and in disturbance of the public peace.

SEDUCE *v.*
1. To draw aside or entice from the path of rectitude and duty in any manner, by flattery, promises, bribes or otherwise; to tempt and lead to iniquity; to corrupt; to deprave.
2. To entice to a surrender of chastity.

SEEK *v.*
1. To go in search or quest of; to look for; to search for by going from place to place.
2. To inquire for; to ask for; to solicit; to endeavor to find or gain by any means.

SEEMLY *a.*
Becoming; fit; suited to the object, occasion, purpose or character; suitable.

SEER *n.*
1. One who sees; as a seer of visions.
2. A prophet; a person who forsees future events.

SEETHE *v.*
To boil; to decoct or prepare for food in hot liquor.

SEIZE *v.*
1. To fall or rush upon suddenly and lay hold on; or to gripe or grasp suddenly.
2. To take possession by force, with or without right.
3. To invade suddenly; to take hold of; to come upon suddenly.

SELAH *n.* (1913)
Supposed to signify silence or a pause.

SELFSAME *a.*
Numerically the same; the very same; identical.

SELFWILLED *a.*
Governed by one's own will; obstinancy.

SELVEDGE *n.*
The edge of a cloth, where it is closed by complicating the threads; a woven border, or border of the close works.

SENSUAL *a.*
1. Carnal; pertaining to the flesh or body, in opposition to the spirit; not spiritual or holy; evil.
2. Pertaining to the senses, as distinct from the mind or soul.
3. Devoted to the gratification of sense; given to the indulgence of the appetites; sewd; luxurious.

SEPULCHRE *n.*
A grave; a tomb; the place in which the dead body of a human being is interred, or a place destined for that purpose.

SERAPHIM *n.*
Angels of the highest order in the celestial hierarchy.

SERJEANT *n.* (Strongs)
A Roman constable or executioner.

SERVANT *n.*
1. One in a state of subjection.
2. A person, male or female, that attends another for the purpose of performing menial offices for him, or who is employed by another for such offices or for other labor, and is subject to his command.

3. A slave; a bondman; one purchased for money, and who was compelled to serve till the year of jubilee; one purchased for a term of years.

4. A person who voluntarily serves another or acts as his minister.

5. A person employed or used as an instrument in accomplishing God's purposes of mercy or wrath.

6. One who yields obedience to another.

SERVE *v.*

1. To work for; to bestow the labor of body and mind in the employment of another.

2. To attend at command; to wait on.

3. To treat; to requite.

4. To obey and worship; to act in conformity to the law of a superior, and treat him with due reverence.

SERVILE *a.*

Such as pertains to a servant or slave; slavish; mean; such as proceeds from dependence.

SERVITOR *n.*

1. A servant; an attendant.

2. One that acts under another; a follower or adherent.

3. One that professes duty and obedience.

SERVITUDE *n.*

The condition of a slave; the state of involuntary subjection to a master; slavery; bondage.

SETTLE *n.*

A seat or bench; something to sit on.

SEVENFOLD *a.*

Repeated seven times; doubled seven times; increased to seven times the size or amount.

SEVER *v.*

1. To part or divide by violence; to separate by parting or rending.

2. To part from the rest by violence.

3. To separate and put in different places or orders.

4. To make a separation or distinction; to distinguish.

SEVERITY *n.*

1. Harshness; rigor; austerity; want of mildness or indulgence.

2. Rigor; extreme strictness.

3. Excessive figor; extreme degree or amount.

4. Extremity; quality or power of distressing.

SHALT
The second person singular of shall.

SHAMBLES *n.*
The place where butcher's meat is sold; a flesh-market.

SHAME *n.*
A painful sensation excited by a consciousness of guilt, or of having done something which injures reputation; or by of that which nature or modesty prompts us to conceal.

SHAMEFACEDNESS *n.*
Bashfulness; excess of modesty.

SHAPE *v.*
To form or create.

SHEAF *n.*
1. A quantity of the stalks of wheat, rye, oats or barley bound together; a bundle of stalks or straw.

2. Any bundle or collection.

SHEAR *v.*
1. To cut or clip something from the surface with an instrument of two blades; to separate any thing from the surface by shears, scissors or a like instrument.

2. To separate by shears.

SHEATH *n.*
A case for the reception of a sword or other long and slender instrument; a scabbard.

SHEAVE *n.*
1. A quantity of the stalks of wheat, rye, oats or barley bound together; a bundle of stalks or straw.

2. Any bundle or collection.

SHEPHERD *n.*
A man employed in tending, feeding and gaurding sheep in the pasture.

SHERD *n.*
A fragment.

SHERIFF *n.*
An officer in each county, to whom is entrusted the

execution of the laws.

SHEW *v.*
1. To exhibit or present to the view of others.
2. To afford to the eye or to notice; to contain in a visible form.
3. To make to know; to cause to understand; to make known; to teach or inform.
4. To inform; to teach.
5. To point out, as a guide.
6. To disclose; to make known.

SHEWBREAD *n.*
Bread of exhibition.

SHIVERS *n.*
A small piece or fragment into which a thing breaks by any sudden violence.

SHOD *past tense of shoe.*

SHONE *v. of shine.*

SHORN *v.*
1. Cut off.
2. Having the hair or wool cut off or sheared.

SHRINE *n.*
A case or box; a case in which sacred things are

deposited.

SHROUD *n.*
1. A shelter; a cover; that which covers, conceals or protects.
2. A branch of a tree.

SHUN *v.*
1. To avoid; to keep clear of; not to fall on or come in contact with.
2. To avoid; not to mix or associate with.
3. To avoid; to decline; to neglect.

SHUTTLE *n.*
An instrument used by weavers for shooting the thread of the woof in weaving from one side of the cloth to the other, between the threads of the warp.

SIEGE *n.*
The setting of an army around or before a fortified place for the purpose of compelling the garrison to surrender; or the surrounding or investing of a place by an army, and approaching it by passages and advanced works, which cover the besiegers from the en-

emy's fire.

SIEGE *v.*
To besiege.

SIEVE *n.*
An utensil for separating flour from bran, or the fine part of any pulverized or fine substance from the coarse, by the hand.

SIFT *v.*
1. To separate by a sieve, as the fine part of a substance from the coarse.
2. To separate; to part.

SIGH *v.*
To inhale a larger quantity of air than usual and immediately expel it; to suffer a single deep respiration.

SIGNET *n.*
A seal.

SIGNIFY *v.*
1. To make known something, either by signs or words.
2. To mean; to have or contain a certain sense.
3. To import; to weigh; to have consequence; used in particular phrases.

4. To make known; to declare.

SILLY *a.*
1. Weak in intellect; foolish; witless; destitute of ordinary strength of mind; simple.
2. Proceeding from want of understanding or common judgment; characterized by weakness of folly; unwise.

SIMILITUDE *n.*
Likeness; resemblance; likeness in nature, qualities of appearance.

SIMPLICITY *n.*
1. Plainness; freedom from subtilty or abstruseness.
2. Artlessness of mind; freedom from a propensity to cunning or stratagem; freedom from duplicity; sincerity.

SIN *n.*
The voluntary departure of a moral agent from a known rule of rectitude or duty, prescribed by God; any voluntary transgression of the divine law, or violation of a divine command; a wicked act; iniq-

uity.

SINCERE *a.*
Being in reality what it appears to be; not feigned; not simulated; not assumed or said for the sake of appearance; real; not hypocritical or pretended.

SINCERITY *n.*
1. Honesty of mind or intention; freedom from simulation or hypocrisy.
2. Freedom from hypocrisy, disguise or false pretense.

SINEW *n.*
A tendon; that which unites a muscle to a bone.

SINFUL *a.*
1. Tainted with sin; wicked; iniquitous; criminal; unholy.
2. Containing sin, or consisting in sin; contrary to the laws of God.

SINGLE *a.*
Pure; simple; incorrupt; unbiased; having clear vision of divine truth.

SINNER *n.*
1. One that has voluntarily violated the divine law; a moral agent who has voluntarily disobeyed any divine precept, or neglected any known duty.
2. An unregenerate person; one who has not received the pardon of his sins.

SITH *adv.*
Since; in later times.

SKIRT *n.*
1. The lower and loose part of a coat or other garment; the part below the waist.
2. The edge of any part of dress.
3. Border; edge; margin; extreme part.

SLAIN *v.*
Killed.

SLANDER *n.*
1. A false tale or report maliciously uttered and tending to injure the reputation of another by lessening him in the esteem of his fellow citizens, by exposing him to impeachment and punishment, or by impairing his means of lining; defamation.
2. Disgrace; reproach; dis-

reputation; ill name.

SLANDER *v.*

To defame; to injure by maliciously uttering a false report respecting one; to tarnish or impair the reputation of one by false tales, maliciously told or propagated.

SLANG *past tense of sling.*

SLAVE *n.*

1. A person who is wholly subject to the will of another; one who has no will of his own, but whose person and services are wholly under the control of another.

2. One who has lost the poser of resistance; or one who surrenders himself to any power whatever.

SLAY *v.*

1. To kill; to put to death by a weapon or by violence.

2. To destroy.

SLEIGHT *n.*

An artful trick; sly artifice; a trick or feat so dexterously performed that the manner of performance escapes observation.

SLEW *past tense of slay.*

SLIGHTLY *adv.*

1. Weakly; superficially; with inconsiderable force or effect; in a small degree.

2. Negligently; without regard.

SLIP *v.*

To escape insensibly; to be lost.

SLOTHFUL *a.*

Inactive; sluggish; lazy; indolent; idle.

SLUGGARD *n.*

A person habitually lazy, idle and inactive; a drone.

SLUICE *n.*

The stream of water issuing through a flood-gate; or the gate itself.

SLUMBER *v.*

1. To sleep lightly; to doze.

2. To sleep.

3. To be in a state of negligence, sloth, supineness or inactivity.

SMART *v.*
1. To feel a pungent pain of mind; to feel sharp pain.
2. To be punished; to bear penalties or the evil consequences of any thing.

SMITE *v.*
1. To strike; to throw, drive or force against; to reach with a blow or a weapon.
2. To kill; to destroy the life of by beating or by weapons of any kind.
3. To afflict; to chasten; to punish.

SMITTEN *v.*
Struck; killed.

SMOTE *past tense of smite.*

SNARE *n.*
Any thing by which one is entangled and brought into trouble.

SNARE *v.*
To catch with a snare; to ensnare; to entangle; to bring into unexpected evil, perplexity or danger.

SNUFF *n.*
The burning part of a can-dle wick, or that which has been charred by the flame, whether burning or not.

SNUFF *v.*
To crop the snuff.

SOBER *a.*
1. Not intoxicated or over-powered by spiritous liq-uors; not drunken.
2. Not mad or insane; not wild, visionary or heated with passion; having the regular exercise of cool dispassionate reason.
3. Regular; calm; not un-der the influence of pas-sion.
4. Serious; solemn; grave.

SOBRIETY *n.*
1. Freedom from intoxica-tion.
2. Habitual freedom from enthusiasm, inordinate passion or overheated imagination; calmness; coolness.
3. Seriousness; gravity.

SOD *n.*
Turf; sward; that stratum of earth on the surface which is filled with the roots of grass, or any por-tion of that surface.

SODDEN *v.*
Boiled; seethed.

SOEVER *so and ever.*

SOJOURN *v.*
To dwell for a time; to dwell or live in a place as a temporary resident, or as a stranger, not considering the place as his permanent habitation.

SOLACE *v.*
1. To cheer in grief or under calamity; to comfort; to relieve in affliction; to console.
2. To allay; to assuage.

SOLACE *v.*
To take comfort; to be cheered or relieved in grief.

SOLE *n.*
The bottom of the foot.

SOLEMN *a.*
1. Anniversary; observed once a year with religious ceremonies.
2. Religiously grave; marked with pomp and sanctity; attended with religious rites.

SOLEMNITY *n.*
1. A rite or ceremony annually performed with religious reverence.
2. A religious ceremony; a ritual performance attended with religious reverence.

SOLEMNLY *adv.*
1. With gravity and religious reverence.
2. With official formalities and be due authority.
3. With religious seriousness.

SOLITARY *a.*
1. Living alone; not having company.
2. Remote from society; not having company, or not much frequented.
3. Lonely; destitute of company.
4. Gloomy; still; dismal.

SOLITARY *n.*
One that lives alone of in solitude; a hermit; a recluse.

SOOTHSAYER *n.*
A foreteller; a prognosticator; one who undertakes to foretell future events without inspiration.

SOP *n.*
1. Anything steeped or dipped and softened in liquor.
2. Something dipped in broth or liquid food, and intended to be eaten.

SORCERER *n.*
A conjurer; an enchanter; a magician.

SORCERY *n.*
Magic; enchantment; witchcraft; divination be the assistance of evil spirits, or the power of commanding evil spirits.

SORE *adv.*
1. With painful violence; intensely; severely; grievously.
2. Greatly; violently; deeply.

SORROW *n.*
The uneasiness or pain of mind which is produced by the loss of any good, or of frustrated hopes of good, or expected loss of happiness; to grieve; to be sad.

SOTTISH *a.*
1. Dull; stupid; senseless; doltish; very foolish.
2. Dull with intemperance.

SOUGHT *past tense of seek.*

SOUL *n.*
1. The spiritual, rational and immortal substance in man, which distinguishes him from brutes; that part of man which enables him to think and reason, and which renders him a subject of moral government.
2. The understanding; the intellectual principle.
3. Vital principle.
4. Spirit; essence; chief part.
5. A human being; a person.
6. Animal life.

SOW *n.*
The female of the hog kind or of swine.

SPAKE *past tense of speak.*

SPED *past tense of speed.*

SPEWING *v.*
Vomiting; ejecting from the stomach.

SPIKENARD *n.*

1. A plant of the genus Nardus.

2. The oil of balsam procured from the spikenard.

SPINDLE *a.*
The pin used in spinning wheels for twisting the thread, and on which the thread when twisted, is wound.

SPIRIT *n.*
1. Primarily, wind; air in motion; breath.

2. The soul of man.

3. An immaterial intelligent being.

4. Temper; disposition of mind, habitual or temporary.

SPIRITUAL *a.*
1. Not fleshly; not material.

2. Pertaining to divine things.

3. Pertaining to spirit or to the affections; pure; holy.

4. Consisting of spirit; not material; incorporeal.

5. Mental; intellectual.

6. Not gross; refined from external things; not sensual.

7. Not lay or temporal; relating to sacred things; ecclesiastical.

8. Pertaining to the renewed nature of man.

SPITE *n.*
Hatred; rancor; malice; malignity; malevolence.

SPITTLE *n.*
Saliva; the thick moist matter which is secreted by the salivary glands and ejected from the mouth.

SPOIL *v.*
1. To plunder; to strip by violence; to rob.

2. To seize by violence; to take by force.

3. To corrupt; to cause to decay and perish.

SPOIL *n.*
1. That which is taken from others by violence.

2. The plunder taken from an enemy; pillage; booty.

3. That which is gained by strength or effort.

SPORT *n.*
1. That which diverts and makes merry; play; game; diversion; mirth.

2. Mock; mockery; contemptuous mirth.

3. That with which one

plays, or which is driven about.

4. Play; idle jingle.

SPORT *v.*
To divert; to make merry.

SPOT *n.*
1. A mark on a substance made by foreign matter; a speck; a blot; a place discolored.
2. A stain on character or reputation; something that soils purity; disgrace; reproach; fault; blemish.

SPRIG *n.*
A small shoot or twig of a tree or other plant; a spray.

SPRUNG *past tense of spring.*

SPUE *v.*
1. To vomit; to puke; to eject from the stomach.
2. To eject; to cast forth.
3. To cast out with abhorrence.

SPUN *past tense of spin.*

STABLISH *v.*
To fix; to settle in a state for permanence; to make firm.

STACTE *n.*
A fatty resinous liquid matter, of the nature of liquid myrrh, very odoriferous and highly valued.

STAGGER *v.*
1. To reel; to vacillate; to move to one side and the other in standing or walking; not to stand or walk with steadiness.
2. To fail; to cease to stand firm; to begin to give way.
3. To hesitate; to begin to doubt and waver in purpose; to become less confident or determined.

STAMMER *v.*
To utter or pronounce with hesitation or imperfectly.

STANCH *v.*
To stop; to set or fix; to stop the flowing of blood.

STANDARD *n.*
An ensign of war; a staff with a flag or colors.

STANDARDBEARER *n.*
An officer of an army, company or troop, that bears a standard.

STATELY *a.*

1. Lofty; dignified; majestic.

2. Magnificent; grand.

STATURE *n.*
The natural heighth of a body.

STATUTE *n.*
An act of the legislature of a state that extends its binding force to all the citizens or subjects; an act of the legislature commanding or prohibiting something; a positive law.

STAVE *n.*
A thin narrow piece of timber, of which casks are made.

STAY *v.*
1. To wait; to attend; to forbear to act.
2. To rest; to rely; to confide in; to trust.
3. To stop from motion or falling; to prop; to hold up; to support.

STAY *n.*
1. Continuance in a place; abode for a time indefinite.
2. Prop; support.

STEAD *n.*

1. Place.
2. Place or room which another had or might have, noting substitution, replacing or filling the place of another.

STEALTH *n.*
1. The act of stealing; theft.
2. Secret act; clandestine practice; means unperceived employed to gain an object; way or manner not perceived.

STEDFAST *a.*
1. Fast fixed; firm; firmly fixed or established.
2. Constant; firm; resolute; not fickle or wavering.

STERN *n.*
The hind part of a ship or other vessel, or of a boat; the part opposite to the stern or prow.

STEWARD *n.*
1. A man employed in great families to manage the domestic concerns, superintend the other servants, collect the rents or income, keep the accounts, &c.
2. A minister of Christ,

whose duty is to dispense the provisions of the gospel, to preach its doctrines and administer its ordinances.

STIFFHEARTED *a.*
Obstinate; stubborn; contumacious.

STIFFNECKED *a.*
Stubborn; inflexibly obstinate; contumacious.

STIR *n.*
Agitation; tumult; bustle; noise or various movements.

STOCK *n.*
1. The stem or main body of a tree or other plant; the fixed, strong, firm part; the origin and support of the branches.
2. The original progenitor; also, the race or line of a family; the progenitors of a family and their direct descendants; lineage; family.
3. The domestic animals or beasts belonging to the owner of a farm.
4. A machine consisting of two pieces of timber, in which the legs of criminals are confined by way of punishment.

STOICK *n.*
A disciple of the philosopher Zeno who taught that men should be free from passion, unmoved by joy or grief, and submit without complaint to the unavoidable necessity by which all things are governed.

STOMACHER *n.*
An ornament or support to the breast, worn by females.

STONE *v.*
To pelt, beat or kill with stones.

STONESQUARERS *n.*
One who forms stones into squares.

STOOP *v.*
1. To bend the body downward and forward.
2. To bend or lean forward; to incline forward in standing or walking.

STOUT *a.*
1. Large; bulky.
2. Proud; resolute; obstinate.

3. Strong; firm.

STRAIGHT *a.*
1. Right; direct; passing from one point to another by the nearest course; not deviating or crooked.
2. Narrow; close; tight.
3. Upright; according with justice and rectitude; not deviating from truth or fairness.

STRAIGHT *adv.*
Immediately; directly; in the shortest time.

STRAIGHTWAY *adv.*
Immediately; without loss of time; without delay.

STRAIN *v.*
1. To stretch; to draw with force; to extend with great effort.
2. To cause to draw with force, or with excess of exertion.
3. To press or cause to pass through some porous substance; to purify or separate from extraneous matter by filtration; to filter.

STRAIT *a.*
1. Narrow; close; not broad.
2. Difficult.

STRAIT *n.*
1. A narrow pass or passage, either in a mountain or in the ocean, between continents or other portions of land.
2. Distress; difficulty; distressing necessity.

STRAITLY *adv.*
1. Narrowly; closely.
2. Strictly; rigorously.
3. Closely; intimately.

STRAKE *past tense of strike.*

STRAKE *n.*
1. A streak.
2. A narrow board.

STRANGLING *n.*
The act of destroying life by stopping respiration.

STRAW *v.*
To spread or scatter.

STRICKEN *v.*
1. Struck; smitten.
2. Advanced; worn; far gone.

STRIFE *n.*

1. Contention in anger or enmity; contest; struggle for victory; quarrel or war.
2. Exertion or contention for superiority; contest of emulation, either by intellectual or physical efforts.
3. Opposition; contrariety; contrast.

STRIKE *v.*
To touch or hit with some force, either with the hand or an instrument; to give a blow to, either with the open hand, the fist, a stick, club or whip, or with a pointed instrument, or with a ball or an arrow discharged.

STRIKER *n.*
1. One that strikes, or that which strikes.
2. A quarrelsome man.

STRIPT *v.*
Pulled or torn off; peeled; skinned; deprived; divested; made naked; impoverished; husked.

STRIVE *v.*
1. To make efforts; to use exertions; to endeavor with earnestness; to labor hard; applicable to exertions of body or mind.
2. To contend; to contest; to struggle in opposition to another; to be in contention or dispute.

STROKE *n.*
1. A blow; the striking of one body against another.
2. A hostile blow or attack.
3. An effort suddenly or unexpectedly produced.

STROVE *past tense of strive.*

STROWED *v.*
Scattered; spread by scattering.

STUBBLE *n.*
The stumps of wheat, rye, barley, oats or buckwheat, left in the ground; the part of the stalk left by the sythe or sickle.

STUBBORNNESS *n.*
1. Perverse and unreasonable obstinacy; inflexibility; contumacy.
2. Stiffness; want of pliancy.

STUDY *n.*
1. A setting of the mind or thoughts upon a subject.

2. Application of mind of books, to arts or science, or to any subject, for the purpose of learning what is not before known.
3. Attention; meditation; contrivance.

STUDY *v.*
1. To fix the mind closely upon a subject; to muse; to dwell upon in thought.
2. To apply the mind to books.
3. To endeavor diligently.

STUMBLE *v.*
1. To trip in walking or moving in any way upon the legs; to strike the foot so as to fall, or to endanger a fall.
2. To err; to slide into a crime or an error.

STUMBLE *n.*
1. A trip in walking or running.
2. A blunder; a failure.

STUMBLINGBLOCK *n.*
Any cause of stumbling; that which causes to err.

SUBDUE *v.*
1. To conquer by force or the exertion of superior power, and bring into permanent subjection; to reduce under dominion.
2. To oppress; to crush; to sink; to overpower so as to disable from further resistance.
3. To tame; to break by conquering a refractory temper or evil passions; to render submissive.

SUBJECT *a.*
1. Placed or situate under.
2. Being under the power and dominion of another.
3. Exposed; liable from extraneous causes.

SUBJECT *n.*
One that owes allegiance to a sovereign and is governed by his laws.

SUBJECT *v.*
1. To bring under the power or dominion of.
2. To put under or within the power of.
3. To submit; to make accountable.
4. To cause to undergo.

SUBJECTION *n.*
1. The act of subduing; the act of vanquishing and bringing under the domin-

ion of another.

2. The state of being under the power, control and government of another.

SUBMIT *v.*

1. To surrender; to yield one's person to the power of another; to give up resistance.

2. To yield one's opinion to the opinion or authority of another.

3. To be subject; to acquiesce in the authority of another.

4. To be submissive; to yield without murmuring.

SUBORN *v.*

To procure a person to take such a false oath as constitutes perjury.

SUBTIL *a.*

1. Sly; artful; cunning; crafty; insinuating.

2. Planned by art; deceitful.

3. Deceitful; treacherous.

SUBTILLY *adv.*

Artfully; cunningly; craftily.

SUBVERT *v.*

1. To overthrow from the

foundation; to overturn; to ruin utterly.

2. To corrupt; to confound; to pervert the mind, and turn it from the truth.

SUCCOUR *v.*

To run to, or run to support; to help or relieve when in difficulty, want or distress; to assist and deliver from suffering.

SUCCOUR *n.*

1. Aid; help; assistance; particularly, assistance that relieves and delivers from difficulty, want or distress.

2. The person or thing that brings relief.

SUCCOURER *n.*

He that affords relief; a helper; a deliverer.

SUFFER *v.*

1. To feel or bear what is painful, disagreeable or distressing, either to the body or mind; to undergo.

2. To endure; to support; to sustain; not to sink under.

3. To allow; to permit; not to forbid or hinder.

SUFFICE *v.*

To be enough or sufficient; to be equal to the end proposed.

SUFFICIENT *a.*
1. Enough; equal to the end proposed; adequate to wants; competent.
2. Qualified; competent; possessing adequate talents or accomplishments.
3. Fit; able; of competent power or ability.

SUMPTUOUSLY *adv.*
Expensively; splendidly; with great magnificence.

SUNDER *v.*
To part; to separate; to divide; to disunite in almost any manner, either by rending, cutting, or breaking.

SUNDER *n.*
In sunder, in two.

SUNDRY *a.*
Several; divers; more than one or two.

SUP *v.*
1. To eat the evening meal.
2. To take into the mouth with the lips.

SUPERFLUITY *n.*
1. Superabundance; a greater quantity than is wanted.
2. Something that is beyond what is wanted; something rendered unnecessary by its abundance.

SUPERFLUOUS *a.*
1. More than is wanted; rendered unnecessary by superabundance.
2. More than sufficient; unnecessary; useless.

SUPERSCRIPTION *n.*
1. That which is written or engraved on the outside, or above something else.
2. An impression of letters on coins.

SUPERSTITION *n.*
1. Excessive exactness or rigor in religious opinions or practice; extreme and unnecessary scruples in the observance of religious rites not commanded, or of points of minor importance; excess or extravagance in religion; the doing of things not required by God, or abstaining from things not forbidden; or the belief of what is absurd, or

belief without evidence.
2. False religion; false worship.

SUPERSTITIOUS *a.*

Over scrupulous and rigid in religious observances; addicted to superstition; full of idle fancies and scruples in regard to religion.

SUPPLANT *v.*

1. To remove or displace by stratagem; or to displace and take the place of.
2. To overthrow; to undermine.

SUPPLE *v.*

To make soft and pliant; to render flexible.

SUPPLIANT *n.*

A humble petitioner; one who entreats submissively.

SUPPLICATION *n.*

1. Entreaty; humble and earnest prayer in worship.
2. Petition; earnest request.

SURETISHIP *n.*

The state of being surety; the obligation of a person to answer for another, and make good any debt or loss which may occur from another's delinquency.

SURETY *n.*

1. Certainty; indubitableness.
2. Security; safety.
3. One that is bound with and for another; one who enters into a bond or recognizance to answer for another's appearance in court, or for his payment of a debt or for the performance of some act, and who, in case of the principal debtor's failure, is compellable to pay the debt or damages.

SURFEIT *v.*

To feed with meat or drink, so as to oppress the stomach and derange the functions of the system; to overfeed and produce sickness or uneasiness.

SURMISING *v.*

Suspecting; imagining upon slight evidence.

SURNAME *n.*

1. An additional name.
2. An appellation added to the original name.

SUSTAIN *v.*
1. To bear; to uphold; to support.
2. To hold; to keep from falling.
3. To support in any condition by aid.

SUSTENANCE *n.*
1. Support; maintenance; subsistence.
2. That which supports life; food; victuals; provisions.

SWADDLE *v.*
To swathe; to bind, as with a bandage; to bind tight with clothes.

SWADDLINGBAND *n.*
A band or cloth wrapped round an infant.

SWARE *past tense of swear.*

SWEAR *v.*
1. To affirm or utter a solemn declaration, with an appeal to God for the truth of what is affirmed.
2. To promise upon oath.

SWELLING *n.*
A tumor, or any morbid enlargement of the natural size.

SWIFT *a.*
1. Moving a great distance or over a large space in a short time; moving with celerity or velocity; fleet; rapid; quick; speedy.
2. Ready; prompt.
3. Speedy; that comes without delay.

SWINE *n.*
A hog, a quadruped of the genus Sus.

SWOON *v.*
To faint; to sink into a fainting fit, in which there is a suspension of the apparent vital functions and mental powers.

SWOON *n.*
A fainting fit; lipothymy; syncope.

SYNAGOGUE *n.*
1. A congregation or assembly of Jews, met for the purpose of worship or the performance of religious rites.
2. The house appropriated to the religious worship of the Jews.
3. The court of the seventy

elders among the Jews, called the great synagogue.

TABERING (Strongs)
To drum.

TABERNACLE *n.*
1. Among the Jews, a movable building, so contrived as to be taken to pieces with ease and reconstructed, for the convenience of being carried during the wanderings of the Israelites in the wilderness.
2. A temporary habitation.
3. Our natural body.
4. God's gracious presence, or the tokens of it.

TABERNACLE *v.*
To dwell; to reside for a time; to be housed.

TABLET *n.*
Something flat on which to write, paint, draw or engrave.

TABRET *n.*
A small drum used as an accompaniment to a pipe or fife.

TACHE *n.*
Something used for taking

hold or holding; a catch; a loop; a button.

TACKLING *n.*
Furniture of the masts and yards of a ship.

TALE *n.*
1. A story; a narrative; the rehearsal of a series of events or adventures, commonly some trifling incidents; or a fictitious narrative.
2. Reckoning; account set down.
3. A telling; information; disclosure of any thing secret.

TALEBEARER *n.*
A person who officiously tells tales; one who impertinently communicates intelligence or anecdotes, and makes mischief in society by his officiousness.

TALENT *n.*
1. A weight, and a coin.
2. A gold coin, the same with a shekel of gold; called also stater, and weighing only four drachmas.
3. The talent of silver, called cicar, was equiva-

lent to three thousand shekels, or one hundred and thirteen pounds, ten ounces and a fraction, troy weight.

TAME *v.*
1. To reclaim; to reduce from a wild to a domestic state; to make gentle and familiar.
2. To civilize.
3. To subdue; to conquer; to depress.

TANNER *n.*
One whose occupation is to tan hides, or convert them into leather by the use of tan.

TAPESTRY *n.*
A kind of woven hangings of wool and silk, often enriched with gold and silver, representing figures of men, animals, landscapes, &c.

TARE *n.*
A weed that grows among corn.

TARGET *n.*
A shield or buckler of a small kind, used as a defensive weapon in war.

TARRY *v.*
1. To stay; to abide; to continue; to lodge.
2. To stay behind.
3. To stay in expectation; to wait.
4. To delay; to put off going or coming; to defer.

TATTLER *n.*
One who tattles; an idle talker; one that tells tales.

TAUNT *v.*
1. To reproach with severe or insulting words; to revile; to upbraid.
2. To exprobrate; to censure.

TAVERN *n.*
A house for the entertainment of travelers.

TEACH *v.*
1. To instruct; to inform; to communicate to another the knowledge of that of which he was before ignorant.
2. To deliver any doctrine, art, principles or words for instruction.
3. To tell; to give intelligence.
4. To accustom; to make familiar.

5. To inform or admonish; to give previous notice to.
6. To suggest to the mind.
7. To counsel and direct.

TEAT *n.*
The projecting part of the female breast; the pap of a woman; the nipple.

TEDIOUS *a.*
1. Wearisome; tiresome from continuance, prolixity, or slowness which causes prolixity.
2. Slow.

TEMPER *v.*
1. To mix so that one part qualifies the other; to bring to a moderate state.
2. To compound; to form by mixture; to qualify, as by an ingredient.
3. To mix, unite or combine two or more things so as to reduce the excess of the qualities of either, and bring the whole to the desired consistence or state.

TEMPERANCE *n.*
1. Moderation; particularly, habitual moderation in regard to the indulgence of the natural appetites and passions; restrained or moderate indulgence.
2. Patience; calmness; sedateness; moderation of passion.

TEMPERATE *a.*
1. Moderate; not excessive.
2. Moderate in the indulgence of the appetites and passions.
3. Cool; calm; not marked with passion; not violent.

TEMPERED *v.*
Duly mixed or modified; reduced to a proper state; softened; allayed; hardened.

TEMPEST *n.*
1. An extensive current of wind, rushing with great velocity and violence; a storm of extreme violence.
2. Perturbation; violent agitation.

TEMPESTUOUS *a.*
1. Very story; turbulent; rough with wind.
2. Blowing with violence.

TEMPLE *n.*
A public edifice erected in honor of some deity.

TEMPORAL *a.*
1. Pertaining to this life or this world or the body only; secular; as temporal concerns; temporal affairs.
2. Measured or limited by time, or by this life or this state of things; having limited existence; opposed to eternal.

TEMPT *v.*
1. To incite or solicit to an evil act; to entice to something wrong by presenting arguments that are plausible or convincing, or by the offer of some pleasure or apparent advantage as the inducement.
2. To provoke; to incite.
3. To solicit; to draw; without the notion of evil.
4. To try; to prove; to put to trial for proof.

TEMPTATION *n.*
1. The act of tempting; enticement to evil by arguments, by flattery, or by the offer of some real or apparent good.
2. Solicitation of the passions; enticements to evil proceeding from the prospect of pleasure or advantage.

3. The state of being tempted or enticed to evil.
4. Trial.

TEMPTED *v.*
Enticed to evil; provoked; tried.

TEMPTER *n.*
1. One that solicits or entices to evil.
2. The great adversary of man; the devil.

TEND *v.*
1. To watch; to guard; to accompany.
2. To hold and take care of.
3. To be attentive to.

TENDER *a.*
1. Soft; easily impressed, broken, bruised or injured; not firm or hard.
2. Very sensible to impression and pain.
3. Delicate; effeminate; not hardy or able to endure hardship.
4. Weak; feeble.
5. Young and carefully educated.
6. Susceptible of the softer passions.
7. Compassionate; easily excited to pity, forgiveness

or favor.

8. Careful to save inviolate, or not to injure.

9. Adapted to excite feeling or sympathy; pathetic.

TENDERHEARTED *a.*

1. Having great sensibility; susceptible of impressions or influence.

2. Very susceptible of the softer passions of love, pity or kindness.

TENON *n.*

In building and cabinet work, the end of a piece of timber, which is fitted to a mortise for insertion, or inserted, for fastening two pieces of timber together.

TENOR *n.*

Sense contained; purport; substance; general course or drift.

TERMED *v.*

Called; denominated.

TERRESTRIAL *a.*

1. Pertaining to the earth; existing on the earth.

2. Consisting of earth.

3. Pertaining to the world, or to the present state; sublunary.

TERRIBLE *a.*

1. Frightful; adapted to excite terror; dreadful; formidable.

2. Adapted to impress dread, terror or solemn awe and reverence.

3. Severely; very; so as to give pain.

TESTAMENT *n.*

1. A solemn authentic instrument in writing, by which a person declares his will as to the disposal of his estate and effects after his death.

2. The name of each general division of the canonical books of the sacred Scriptures.

TESTATOR *n.*

A man who makes and leaves a will or testament at death.

TESTIFY *v.*

1. To make a solemn declaration, verbal or written, to establish some fact; to give testimony for the purpose of communicating to others a knowledge of something not known to them.

2. In judicial proceedings,

to make a solemn declaration under oath, for the purpose of establishing or making proof of some act to a court.
3. To declare a charge against one.
4. To bear witness to; to support the truth of by testimony.
5. To publish and declare freely.

THANKWORTHY *a.*
Deserving thanks; meritorious.

THEATRE *n.*
An edifice in which spectacles or shows were exhibited for the amusement of spectators.

THEE *pron. obj. case of thou.*

THEE *v.*
To thrive; to prosper.

THENCE *adv.*
1. From that place.
2. From that time.

THEREABOUT *adv.*
Concerning that.

THEREAT *adv.*

1. At that place.
2. At that thing or event; on that account.

THERETO *adv.*
To that or this.

THICKET *n.*
A wood or collection of trees or shrubs closely set.

THINE *adj.*
Thy; belonging to thee; relating to thee; being the property of thee.

THISTLE *n.*
The common name of numerous prickly plants.

THITHER *adv.*
1. To that place; opposed to hither.
2. To that end or point.

THITHERWARD *adv.*
Toward that place.

THONG *n.*
A strap of leather, used for fastening any thing.

THOU *pron.*
The second personal pronoun, in the singular number; the pronoun which is used in addressing persons

in the solemn style.

impel.

THREESCORE *a.*
Thrice twenty; sixty; as
threescore years.

THRESH *v.*
1. To beat out grain from
the husk or pericarp with a
flail.
2. To beat corn off from
the cob or spike.
3. To beat soundly with a
stick or whip; to drub.

THREW *past tense of
throw.*

THRICE *adv.*
Three times.

THRONG *n.*
1. A crowd; a multitude of
persons or of living beings
pressing or pressed into a
close body or assemblage.
2. A great multitude.

THRONG *v.*
To crowd or press; to op-
press or annoy with a
crowd of living beings.

THRUST *v.*
1. To push or drive with
force.
2. To drive; to force; to

THUMMIM *n.*
A Hebrew word denoting
perfections. The Urim and
Thummim were worn in
the breastplate of the high
priest, but what they were,
has never been satisfacto-
rily ascertained.

TIDINGS *n.*
News; advice; information;
intelligence; account of
what has taken place, and
was not before known.

TILLAGE *n.*
The operation, practice or
art of preparing land for
seed, and keeping the
ground free from weeds
which might impede the
growth of crops.

TILLER *n.*
A money box in a shop; a
drawer.

TILL *v.*
To labor; to cultivate; to
plow and prepare for seed,
and to dress crops.

TIMBREL *n.*
An instrument of music; a
kind of drum, tabor or tab-

ret, which has been in use from the highest antiquity.

TIRE *n.*
A head dress; something that encompasses the head.

TITHE *n.*
The tenth part of any thing.

TITHE *v.*
To levy a tenth part on; to tax to the amount of a tenth.

TITTLE *n.*
A small particle; a minute part; a jot; an iota.

TOIL *v.*
To labor; to work; to exert strength with pain and fatigue of body or mind, with efforts of some continuance or duration.

TOIL *n.*
Labor with pain and fatigue; labor that oppresses the body or mind.

TOKEN *n.*
1. A sign; something intended to represent or indicate another thing or an event.
2. A mark.

TOLERABLE *a.*
1. That may be borne or endured; supportable, either physically or mentally.
2. Moderately good or agreeable; not contemptible; not very excellent or pleasing, but such as can be borne or received without disgust, resentment or opposition.

TOLL *n.*
A tax paid for some liberty or privilege.

TOMB *n.*
1. A grave; a pit in which the dead body of a human being is deposited.
2. A house or vault formed wholly or partly in the earth, with walls and a roof for the reception of the dead.
3. A monument erected to preserve the memory of the dead.

TORMENT *n.*
1. Extreme pain; anguish; the utmost degree of misery, either of body or mind.
2. That which gives pain, vexation or misery.

TORTURED *v.*
Tormented; stretched on
the wheel; harassed.

TOTTER *v.*
1. To shake so as to
threaten a fall; to vacillate.
2. To reel; to lean.

TOW *n.*
The coarse and broken part
of flax or hemp, separated
from the finer part by the
hatchel or swingle.

TOWARD *prep.*
1. In the direction to.
2. With direction to; with
respect to; regarding.

TRADITION *n.*
1. Delivery; the act of de-
livering into the hands of
another.
2. The delivery of opinions, doctrines, practices,
rites and customs from father to son, or from ancestors to posterity; the trans-
mission of any opinions or
practice from forefathers
to descendants by oral
communication, without
written memorials.
3. That which is handed
down from age to age by
oral communication.

THY *a.*
The adjective of thou, or a
pronominal adjective, signifying of thee, or belonging to thee.

TRAITOR *n.*
1. One who violates his
allegiance.
2. One who betrays his
trust.

TRAMPLE *v.*
1. To tread under foot; especially, to tread upon
with pride, contempt, tri-
umph or scorn.
2. To tread down; to pros-
trate by treading.
3. To treat with pride, contempt and insult.

TRANCE *n.*
An ecstasy; a state in
which the soul seems to
have passed out of the
body into celestial regions,
or to be rapt into visions.

TRANQUILLITY *n.*
Quietness; a calm state;
freedom from disturbance
or agitation.

TRANSFIGURED *v.*
Changed in form.

TRANSFORMED *v.*
Changed in form or external appearance; metamorphosed; transmuted; renewed.

TRANSGRESS *v.*
1. To pass over or beyond any limit; to surpass.
2. To overpass any rule prescribed as the limit of duty; to break or violate a law, civil or moral.

TRANSGRESS *v.*
To offend by violating a law; to sin.

TRANSGRESSION *n.*
The act of passing over or beyond any law or rule of moral duty; the violation of a law or known principle of rectitude; breach of command.

TRANSGRESSOR *n.*
One who breaks a law or violates a command; one who violates any known rule or principle of rectitude; a sinner.

TRANSLATE *v.*
1. To bear, carry or remove from one place to another.

2. To remove or convey to heaven.
3. To transfer; to convey from one to another.

TRAVAIL *v.*
1. To labor with pain; to toil.
2. To suffer the pangs of childbirth; to be in labor.

TRAVERSING *v.*
Crossing; passing over; thwarting; turning; denying.

TREACHEROUS *a.*
Violating allegiance of faith pledged; faithless; betraying a trust.

TREACHERY *n.*
Violation of allegiance or of faith and confidence.

TREAD *v.*
1. To set the foot.
2. To walk or go.
3. To tread or tread on, to trample; to set the foot on in contempt.
4. To press out with the feet; to press out wine or wheat.

TREASON *n.*
The offense of attempting

to overthrow the government of the state to which the offender owes allegiance.

TREASURE *n.*
1. Wealth accumulated; particularly, a stock or store of money in reserve.
2. A great quantity of any thing collected for future use.
3. Something very much valued.
4. Great abundance.

TREASURE *v.*
To hoard; to collect and reposit, either money or other things, for future use; to lay up.

TREATISE *n.*
A tract; a written composition on a particular subject, in which the principles of it are discussed or explained.

TREMBLE *v.*
To shake involuntarily; to quake; to quiver; to shiver; to shudder.

TRESPASS *v.*
1. To pass beyond.
2. To commit any offense or to do any act that injures or annoys another; to violate any rule of rectitude to the injury of another.
3. To transgress voluntarily any divine law or command; to violate any known rule of duty.

TRESPASS *n.*
1. Any injury or offense done to another.
2. Any voluntary transgression of the moral law; any violation of a known rule of duty; sin.

TRIBULATION *n.*
1. Severe affliction; distresses of life; vexations.
2. The troubles and distresses which proceed from persecution.

TRIBUTARY *n.*
One that pays tribute or a stated sum to a conquering power, for the purpose of securing peace and protection, or as an acknowledgment of submission, or for the purchase of security.

TRIBUTE *n.*
1. An annual or stated sum of money or other valuable thing, paid by one prince

or nation to another, either as an acknowledgment of submission, or as the price of peace and protection, or by virtue of some treaty.
2. Something given or contributed.

TRODDEN *v.*
Jerusalem shall be trodden down by the Gentiles.

TRODE *past tense of tread.*

TRODE *n.*
Tread; footing.

TROUBLOUS *a.*
1. Agitated; tumultuous; full of commotion.
2. Full of trouble or disorder; full of affliction.

TROUGH *n.*
1. A vessel hollow longitudinally, or a large log or piece of timber excavated longitudinally on the upper side; used for various purposes.
2. A tray.
3. The channel that conveys water.

TROW *v.*
To believe; to trust; to

think or suppose.

TRUCEBREAKER *n.*
One who violates a truce, covenant or engagement.

TRUE *a.*
1. Conformable to fact; being in accordance with the actual state of things.
2. Genuine; pure; real; not counterfeit, adulterated or false.
3. Free from falsehood.
4. Straight; right.

TRUMP *n.*
A trumpet; a wind instrument of music; a poetical word used for trumpet.

TRUST *n.*
1. Confidence; a reliance or resting of the mind on the integrity, veracity, justice, friendship or other sound principle of another person.
2. He or that which is the ground of confidence.
3. That which is committed to one's care.

TRUST *v.*
1. To place confidence in; to rely on.
2. To believe; to credit.

3. To be confident of something present or future.
4. To be credulous; to be won to confidence.
5. To commit to the care of, in confidence.

TRUTH *n.*
1. Conformity to fact or reality; exact accordance with that which is, or has been, or shall be.
2. Conformity of words to thoughts, which is called moral truth.
3. Veracity; purity from falsehood; practice of speaking truth; habitual disposition to speak truth.
4. Correct opinion.
5. Jesus Christ.

TUMULT *n.*
1. The commotion, disturbance or agitation of a multitude.
2. Violent commotion or agitation with confusion of sounds.
3. Agitation; high excitement; irregular or confused motion.
4. Bustle; stir.

TUMULTUOUS *a.*
1. Greatly agitated; irregu-

lar; noisy; confused.
2. Agitated; disturbed.
3. Turbulent; violent.
4. Full of tumult and disorder.

TURTLE *n.*
A fowl of the genus Columba; called also the turtle dove, and turtle pigeon.

TUTOR *n.*
1. A guardian; one who has the charge of a child or pupil and his estate.
2. One who has the care of instructing another in various branches or in any branch of human learning.

TUTOR *v.*
1. To teach; to instruct.
2. To treat with authority or severity.
3. To correct.

TWAIN *a.*
Two.

TWILIGHT *n.*
The faint light which is reflected upon the earth after sunset and before sunrise; crepuscular light.

TWINE *v.*

1. To twist; to wind.
2. To unite closely; to cling to; to embrace.
3. To gird; to wrap closely about.

TWINE *n.*
A strong thread composed of two or three smaller threads or strands twisted together.

TWOFOLD *adv.*
Doubly; in a double degree.

UNBELIEF *n.*
1. Incredulity; the withholding of belief.
2. Infidelity; disbelief of divine revelation.
3. Disbelief of the truth of the gospel, rejection of Christ as the Savior of men, and of the doctrines he taught; distrust of God's promises and faithfulness, &c.
4. Weak faith.

UNBELIEVER *n.*
1. An incredulous person; one who does not believe.
2. An infidel; one who discredits revelation, or the mission, character and doctrines of Christ.

UNBLAMEABLE *a.*
Not blamable; not culpable; innocent.

UNCLEAN *a.*
1. Not clean; foul; dirty; filthy.
2. Ceremonially impure; not cleansed by ritual practices.
3. Foul with sin.
4. Not in covenant with God.
5. Lewd; unchaste.

UNCOMELY *a.*
1. Not comely; wanting grace.
2. Unseemly; unbecoming; unsuitable.

UNCONDEMNED *a.*
1. Not condemned; not judged guilty.
2. Not disapproved; not pronounced criminal.

UNCORRUPTIBLE *a.*
That cannot be corrupted.

UNCTION *n.*
Divine or sanctifying grace.

UNDEFILED *a.*
Not defiled; not polluted; not vitiated.

UNDERGIRD *v.*
To bind below; to gird round the bottom.

UNDERSETTER *n.*
A prop; a pedestal; a support.

UNDERTAKE *v.*
1. To engage in; to enter upon; to take in hand; to begin to perform.
2. To covenant or contract to perform or execute.

UNFAITHFUL *a.*
1. Not observant of promises, vows, allegiance or duty; violating trust or confidence; treacherous; perfidious.
2. Not performing the proper duty.
3. Impious; infidel.
4. Negligent of duty.

UNFEIGNED *a.*
Not feigned; not counterfeit; not hypocritical; real; sincere.

UNFRUITFUL *a.*
1. Not producing fruit; barren.
2. Not producing offspring; not prolific; barren.
3. Not producing good effects or works.
4. Unproductive; not fertile.

UNGIRDED *v.*
Loosed from a girth or band.

UNGODLY *a.*
1. Wicked; impious; neglecting the fear and worship of God, or violating his commands.
2. Sinful; contrary to the divine commands.
3. Polluted by wickedness.

UNHOLY *a.*
1. Not holy; not renewed and sanctified.
2. Profane; not hallowed; not consecrated; common.
3. Impious; wicked.
4. Not ceremonially purified.

UNICORN *n.*
An animal with one horn; the monoceros.

UNITY *n.*
1. The state of being one; oneness.
2. Concord; conjunction.
3. Agreement.
4. Oneness of sentiment, affection or behavior.

5. The oneness which subsists between Christ and his saints, by which the same spirit dwells in both, and both have the same disposition and aims.

UNJUST *a.*
1. Not just; acting contrary to the standard of right established by the divine law; not equitable.
2. Contrary to justice and right; wrongful.

UNLADE *v.*
1. To unload; to take out the cargo of.
2. To unload; to remove.

UNLEARNED *v.*
1. Forgotten.
2. Not learned; ignorant; illiterate; not instructed.
3. Not gained by study; not known.

UNMERCIFUL *a.*
1. Not merciful; cruel; inhuman to such beings as are in one's power; not disposed to spare or forgive.
2. Unconscionable; exorbitant.

UNMINDFUL *a.*
Not mindful; not heedful; not attentive; regardless.

UNMOVEABLE *a.*
That cannot be moved or shaken; firm; fixed.

UNPERFECT *a.*
Not perfect; not complete.

UNPROFITABLE *a.*
1. Bringing no profit; producing no gain beyond the labor, expenses and interest of capital.
2. Producing no improvement or advantage; useless; serving no purpose.
3. Not useful to others.
4. Misimproving talents; bringing no glory to God.

UNQUENCHABLE *a.*
That cannot be quenched; that will never be extinguished; inextinguishable.

UNREPROVEABLE *a.*
Not deserving reproof; that cannot be justly censured.

UNRIGHTEOUS *a.*
1. Not righteous; not just; not conformed in heart and life to the divine law; evil; wicked.
2. Unjust; contrary to law and equity.

UNRULY *a.*
Disregarding restraint; licentious; disposed to violate laws; turbulent; ungovernable.

UNSATIABLE *a.*
That cannot be satisfied.

UNSAVOURY *a.*
1. Tasteless; having no taste.
2. Having a bad taste or smell.
3. Unpleasing; disgusting.

UNSEEMLY *a.*
Not fit or becoming; uncomely; unbecoming; indecent.

UNSEEMLY *adv.*
Indecently; unbecomingly.

UNSHOD *a.*
Not shod; having no shoes.

UNSPOTTED *a.*
1. Not stained; free from spot.
2. Free from moral stain; untainted with guilt; unblemished; immaculate.

UNSTABLE *a.*
1. Not stable; not fixed.
2. Not steady; inconstant;

irresolute; wavering.

UNTHANKFUL *a.*
Not thankful; ungrateful; not making acknowledgments for good received.

UNTIMELY *a.*
1. Happening before the usual time.
2. Happening before the natural time; premature.

UNTOWARD *a.*
Froward; perverse; refractory; not easily guided or taught.

UNWISE *a.*
1. Not wise; not choosing the best means for the end; defective in wisdom.
2. Not dictated by wisdom; not adapted to the end.

UNWORTHY *a.*
1. Not deserving.
2. Not deserving; wanting merit.
3. Unbecoming; vile; base.
4. Not suitable; inadequate.

UPBRAID *v.*
1. To charge with something wrong or disgraceful; to reproach; to cast in the

teeth.

2. To reproach; to chide.

3. To reprove with severity.

UPHOLD *v.*

1. To lift on high; to elevate.

2. To support; to sustain; to keep from falling or slipping.

UPRIGHT *a.*

1. Honest; just; adhering to rectitude in all social intercourse; not deviating from correct moral principles.

2. Conformable to moral rectitude.

3. Erect; perpendicular to the plane of the horizon.

UPRISING *n.*

The act of rising.

USURER *n.*

1. A person who lent money and took interest for it.

2. In present usage, one who lends money at a rate of interest beyond the rate established by law.

USURP *v.*

To seize and hold in possession by force or without right.

USURY *n.*

1. Interest; a premium paid or stipulated to be paid for the use of money.

2. The practice of taking interest.

UTMOST *a.*

1. Extreme; being at the furthest point or extremity.

2. Being in the greatest or highest degree.

UTMOST *n.*

The most that can be; the greatest power, degree or effort.

UTTER *a.*

1. Situated on the outside or remote from the center.

2. Placed or being beyond any compass; out of any place.

3. Extreme; excessive; utmost.

4. Complete; total; final.

UTTER *v.*

To speak; to pronounce; to express.

UTTERANCE *n.*

1. The act of uttering words; pronunciation;

manner of speaking.
2. Emission from the mouth; vocal expression.

UTTERLY *adv.*
To the full extent; fully; perfectly; totally.

UTTERMOST *a.*
Extreme; being in the furthest, greatest or highest degree.

UTTERMOST *n.*
The greatest.

VAIL *n.*
1. Any kind of cloth which is used for intercepting the view and hiding something.
2. A piece of thin cloth or silk stuff, used by females to hide their faces.
3. A cover; that which conceals.

VAIL *v.*
To cover; to hide from the sight.

VAIN *a.*
1. Empty; worthless; having no substance, value or importance.
2. Fruitless; ineffectual.
3. Proud of petty things, or

of trifling attainments.
4. False; deceitful; not genuine; spurious.
5. Not effectual; having no efficacy.

VAINGLORY *n.*
Exclusive vanity excited by one's own performances; empty pride; undue elation of mind.

VALE *n.*
A tract of low ground or of land between hills; a valley.

VALIANT *a.*
1. Primarily, strong; vigorous in body.
2. Brave; courageous; intrepid in danger; heroic.
3. Performed with valor; bravely conducted; heroic.

VALOUR *n.*
Strength of mind in regard to danger; that quality which enables a man to encounter danger with firmness; personal bravery; courage; intrepidity; prowess.

VANITY *n.*
1. Emptiness; want of substance to satisfy desire;

uncertainty; inanity.

2. Fruitless desire or endeavor.

3. Inflation of mind upon slight grounds; empty pride, inspired by an overweening conceit of one's personal attainments or decorations.

VAPOUR *n.*

1. An invisible elastic fluid, rendered aeriform by heat, and capable of being condensed, or brought back to the liquid or solid state, by cold.

2. Something unsubstantial, fleeting or transitory.

VARIABLENESS *n.*

1. Susceptibility of change; liableness or aptness to alter; changeableness.

2. Inconstancy; fickleness; unsteadiness; levity.

VARIANCE *n.*

1. In a state of dissension or controversy; in a state of enmity.

2. In disagreement; in a state of difference or want of agreement.

VAUNT *v.*

To boast; to make a vain display of one's own worth, attainments or decorations; to talk with vain ostentation; to brag.

VEHEMENT *a.*

1. Violent; acting with great force; furious; very forcible.

2. Very ardent; very eager or urgent; very fervent.

VEIL *n.*

1. A cover; a curtain; something to intercept the view and lude an object.

2. A cover; a disguise.

VEIL *v.*

1. To cover with a veil; to conceal.

2. To invest; to cover.

3. To hide.

VENGEANCE *n.*

The infliction of pain on another, in return for an injury or offense.

VENISON *n.*

The flesh of beasts of game, or of such wild animals as are taken in the chase.

VENTURE *n.*

1. An undertaking of chance or danger; the risking of something upon an event which cannot be foreseen with tolerable certainty.
2. Chance; hap; contingency; luck; an event that is not or cannot be foreseen.

VERILY *adv.*
1. In truth; in fact; certainly.
2. Really; truly; with great confidence.

VERITY *n.*
1. Truth; consonance of a statement, proposition or other thing to fact.
2. Moral truth; agreement of the words with the thoughts.

VERMILION *a.*
Red sulphuret of mercury; a bright, beautiful red color of two sorts, natural and artificial.

VESSEL *n.*
1. A cask or utensil proper for holding liquors and other things, as a tun, a pipe, a puncheon, a hogshead, a barrel, a firkin, a bottle, a kettle, a cup, a dish, &c.
2. Any building used in navigation, which carries masts and sails, from the largest ship of war down to a fishing sloop.
3. Something containing.

VESTMENT *n.*
A garment; some part of clothing or dress.

VESTRY *n.*
A room in which sacerdotal vestments and sacred utensils are kept.

VESTURE *n.*
1. A garment; a robe.
2. Clothing; covering.

VEX *v.*
1. To irritate; to make angry by little provocations.
2. To plague; to torment; to harass; to afflict.
3. To disturb; to disquiet; to agitate.
4. To trouble; to distress.
5. To persecute.

VEXATION *n.*
1. The act of irritation, or of troubling, disquieting and harassing.
2. State of being irritated

or disturbed in mind.
3. Disquiet; agitation;
great uneasiness.
4. Afflictions; great troubles; severe judgments.

VIAL *n.*
A small bottle of thin
glass, used particularly by
apothecaries and druggists.

VICTORY *n.*
1. The advantage or superiority gained over spiritual enemies, over passions
and appetites, or over
temptations, or in any
struggle or competition.
2. Conquest; the defeat of
an enemy in battle, or of
an antagonist in contest; a
gaining of the superiority
in war or combat.

VICTUAL *n.*
Food for human beings,
prepared for eating; that
which supports human life;
provisions; meat; sustenance.

VIGILANT *a.*
Watchful; circumspect;
attentive to discover and
avoid danger, or to provide
for safety.

VILE *a.*
1. Base; mean; worthless;
despicable.
2. Morally base or impure;
sinful; depraved by sin;
wicked; hateful in the sight
of God and of good men.

VILLANY *n.*
1. Extreme depravity; atrocious wickedness.
2. A crime; an action of
deep depravity.

VINEDRESSER *n.*
One who dresses, trims,
prunes and cultivates
vines.

VINTAGE *n.*
1. The produce of the vine
for the season.
2. The time of gathering
the crop of grapes.

VIOL *n.*
A stringed musical instrument, of the same form as
the violin, but larger, and
having six strings, to be
struck with a bow.

VIOLATE *v.*
1. To injure; to hurt; to
interrupt; to disturb.
2. To break; to infringe; to
transgress.

3. To injure; to do violence to.

4. To treat with irreverence; to profane.

VIOLENCE *n.*
1. Physical force; strength of action or motion.
2. Moral force; vehemence.
3. Outrage; unjust force; crimes of all kinds.
4. Injury; hurt.

VIPER *n.*
1. A serpent, a species of coluber, whose bite is remarkably venomous.
2. A person or thing mischievous or malignant.

VIRGIN *n.*
A woman who has had no carnal knowledge of man.

VIRGINITY *n.*
Maidenhood; the state of having had no carnal knowledge of man.

VIRTUE *n.*
1. Moral goodness; the practice of moral duties and the abstaining from vice, or a conformity of life and conversation to the moral law.

2. A particular moral excellence.
3. Strength; that substance or quality of physical bodies, by which they act and produce effects on other bodies.

VIRTUOUS *a.*
1. Morally good; acting in conformity to the moral law; practicing the moral duties, and abstaining from vice.
2. Being in conformity to the moral or divine law.
3. Chaste.

VISAGE *n.*
The face; the countenance or look of a person.

VISITATION *n.*
1. The act of visiting.
2. The sending of afflictions and distresses on men to punish them for their sins, or to prove them.

VOCATION *n.*
1. A calling by the will of God.
2. Summons; call; inducement.

VOID *a.*
1. Having no legal or bind-

ing force; null; not effectual to bind parties, or to
convey or support a right;
not sufficient to produce
its effect.
2. Empty; vacant; not occupied with any visible
matter.
3. Free; clear.
4. Destitute.
5. To make void; to violate; to transgress.
6. To render useless or of
no effect.

VOID *n.*
An empty space.

VOW *n.*
1. A solemn promise made
to God, or by a pagan to
his deity.
2. A solemn promise.

VOW *v.*
1. To give, consecrate or
dedicate to God by a sol-
emn promise.
2. To devote.

WAIL *v.*
1. To lament; to moan; to
bewail.
2. To weep; to express sorrow audibly.

WAILING *n.*

Loud cries of sorrow; deep
lamentation.

WALLOW *v.*
To roll ones body.

WALLOW *n.*
A kind of rolling walk.

WANTON *a.*
1. Wandering from moral
rectitude; licentious; dissolute; indulging in sensual-
ity without restraint.
2. More appropriately, deviating from the rules of
chastity; lewd; lustful; lascivious; libidinous.
3. Disposed to unchastity;
indicating wantonness.
4. Loose; unrestrained;
running to excess.

WARD *n.*
Custody; confinement un-
der guard.

WARDROBE *n.*
Wearing apparel.

WARE *past tense of wear.*

WARE *n.*
Goods; commodities; mer-
chandise.

WASTER *n.*

One who is prodigal; one who squanders property; one who consumes extravagantly or without use.

WATCH *n.*
1. A period of the night, in which one person or one set of persons stand as sentinels; the time from one relief of sentinels to another.
2. A watchman, or watchmen; men set for a guard, either one person or more, set to espy the approach of an enemy or other danger, and to give an alarm or notice of such danger; a sentinel; a guard.
3. Attention; close observation.
4. Guard; vigilance for keeping or protecting against danger.

WATCH *v.*
1. To be attentive; to be vigilant in preparation for an event or trial, the time of whose arrival is uncertain.
2. To look with expectation.
3. To be attentive; to look with attention or steadiness.

4. To keep guard; to act as sentinel; to look for danger.

WATCHFUL *a.*
Vigilant; attentive; careful to observe; observant; cautious.

WATCHMAN *n.*
A sentinel; a guard.

WATCHTOWER *n.*
A tower on which a sentinel is placed to watch for enemies or the approach of danger.

WAX *v.*
To pass from one state to another; to become.

WAXEN *a.*
Made of wax; as waxen cells.

WAYFARING *a.*
Traveling; passing; being on a journey.

WAYSIDE *n.* (1913)
The side of the way; the edge or border of a road or path.

WEALTH *v.*
Prosperity; external happi-

ness.

WEANED *v.*
Accustomed or reconciled to the want of the breast or other object of desire.

WEARISOME *a.*
Causing weariness; tiresome; tedious; fatiguing.

WEARY *a.*
1. Having the strength much exhausted by toil or violent exertion; tired; fatigued.
2. Having the patience exhausted, or the mind yielding to discouragement.

WEARY *v.*
To reduce or exhaust the physical strength of the body; to tire; to fatigue.

WEDLOCK *n.*
Marriage; matrimony.

WEDLOCK *v.*
To marry.

WEN *n.*
An encysted swelling or tumor; a fleshy excrescence growing on animals.

WHELP *n.*
The young of the canine species.

WHENCE *adv.*
1. From what place.
2. From what source.
3. From which premises, principles or facts.

WHENSOEVER *adv.*
At what time soever; at whatever time.

WHEREABOUT *adv.*
1. Near what place.
2. Near which place.
3. Concerning which.

WHEREFORE *adv.*
1. For which reason.
2. Why; for what reason.

WHEREINTO *adv.*
Into which.

WHEREOF *adv.*
1. Of which.
2. Of what.

WHEREON *adv.*
1. On which.
2. On what.

WHERETO *adv.*
1. To which.
2. To what; to what end.

WHEREWITH *adv.*
1. With which.
2. With what, interrogatively.

WHEREWITHAL *adv.*
The same as wherewith.

WHET *v.*
To rub for the purpose of sharpening, as an edge tool; to sharpen by attrition.

WHIT *n.*
A point; a jot; the smallest part or particle imaginable.

WHOLESOME *a.*
1. Tending to promote health; favoring health; salubrious.
2. Sound; contributing to the health of the mind; favorable to morals, religion or prosperity.

WHOLLY *adv.*
1. Entirely; completely; perfectly.
2. Totally; in all the parts or kinds.

WHORE *n.*
A harlot; a courtesan; a concubine; a prostitute.

WHORE *v.*
1. To have unlawful sexual commerce; to practice lewdness.
2. To corrupt by lewd intercourse.

WHOREDOM *n.*
1. Lewdness; fornication; practice of unlawful commerce with the other sex.
2. Idolatry; the desertion of the worship of the true God, for the worship of idols.

WHOREMONGER *n.*
One who practices lewdness.

WHORISH *a.*
Lewd; unchaste; addicted to unlawful sexual pleasures; incontinent.

WHOSO *pron.*
Any person whatever.

WICKED *a.*
1. Persons who live in sin; transgressors of the divine law; all who are unreconciled to God, unsanctified or impenitent.
2. Evil in principle or practice; deviating from the divine law; addicted to

vice; sinful; immoral.
3. Cursed; baneful; pernicious.

WICKEDNESS *n.*
Departure from the rules of the divine law; evil disposition or practices; immorality; crime; sin; sinfulness; corrupt manners.

WILE *n.*
A trick or stratagem practiced for ensnaring or deception; a sly, insidious artifice.

WILFULLY *adv.*
1. By design; with set purpose.
2. Obstinately; stubbornly.

WILL *n.*
1. That faculty of the mind by which we determine either to do or forbear an action; the faculty which is exercised in deciding, among two or more objects, which we shall embrace or pursue.
2. Choice; determination. It is my will to prosecute the trespasser.
3. Command; direction.
4. Power; arbitrary disposal.

WILT *v.*
To wish; to be inclined to.

WIMPLE *n.*
A hood or vail.

WIMPLE *v.*
To draw down, as a vail.

WINEBIBBER *n.*
One who drinks much wine; a great drinker.

WINNOW *v.*
To separate and drive off the chaff from grain by means of wind.

WIS *v.*
To think; to suppose; to imagine.

WISDOM *n.*
1. The right use or exercise of knowledge; the choice of laudable ends, and of the best means to accomplish them.
2. The exercise of sound judgment either in avoiding evils or attempting good.
3. True religion; godliness; piety; the knowledge and fear of God, and sincere and uniform obedience to his commands.

4. Quickness of intellect; readiness of apprehension; dexterity in execution.
5. Human learning; erudition; knowledge of arts and sciences.
6. Natural instinct and sagacity.
7. Profitable words or doctrine.

WIST *past tense of wis.*

WIT *v.*
To know.

WITCH *n.*
1. A woman who by compact with the devil, practices sorcery or enchantment.
2. A woman who is given to unlawful arts.

WITCHCRAFT *n.*
The practices of witches; sorcery; enchantments; intercourse with the devil.

WITHAL *adv.*
With the rest; together with; likewise; at the same time.

WITHDRAW *v.*
1. To take back; to take from.

2. To recall; to cause to retire or leave; to call back or away.

WITHER *v.*
1. To fade; to lose its native freshness; to become sapless; to dry.
2. To waste; to pine away.

WITHHOLD *v.*
1. To hold back; to restrain; to keep from action.
2. To retain; to keep back; not to grant.

WITHOUT *prep.*
1. On the outside of.
2. Beyond; not within.

WITNESS *n.*
1. Testimony; attestation of a fact or event.
2. That which furnishes evidence or proof.
3. A person who knows or sees any thing; one personally present.
4. One who gives testimony.

WITNESS *v.*
1. To attest; to give testimony to; to testify to something.
2. To give evidence.

WITS *n.*
Soundness of mind; intellect not disordered.

WITTINGLY *adv.*
Knowingly; with knowledge; by design.

WITTY *a.*
1. Possessed of wit; full of wit.
2. Judicious; ingenious; inventive.

WIZARD *n.*
A conjurer; an enchanter; a sorcerer.

WOE *n.* (1913)
1. Grief; sorrow; misery; heavy calamity
2. A curse; a malediction.

WOEFUL *a.* (Strongs)
Desperately incurable or sick.

WOMB *n.*
1. The uterus or matrix of a female.
2. The place where any thing is produced.
3. Any large or deep cavity.

WONT *a.*
Accustomed; habituated;
using or doing customarily.

WONT *v.*
To be accustomed or habituated; to be used.

WOOF *n.*
1. The threads that cross the warp in weaving; the weft.
2. Texture; cloth; as a pall of softest woof.

WORLDLY *a.*
1. Secular; temporal; pertaining to this world or life, in contradistinction to the life to come.
2. Devoted to this life and its enjoyments; bent on gain.

WORSHIP *n.*
1. The act of paying divine honors to the Supreme Being; or the reverence and homage paid to him in religious exercises, consisting in adoration, confession, prayer, thanksgiving and the like.
2. Honor; respect; civil deference.
3. Excellence of character; dignity; worth; worthiness.
4. A term of ironical re-

spect.

WORSHIP *v.*
1. To adore; to pay divine honors to; to reverence with supreme respect and veneration.
2. To perform acts of adoration.
3. To perform religious service.

WORST *a.*
1. Most bad; most evil; in a moral sense.
2. Most severe or dangerous; most difficult to heal.
3. Most afflictive, pernicious or calamitous.

WORTHY *a.*
1. Deserving; such as merits; having worth or excellence.
2. Possessing worth or excellence of qualities; virtuous; estimable.

WOT *v.*
To know; to be aware.

WRATH *n.*
1. Violent anger; vehement exasperation; indignation.
2. The effects of anger.
3. The just punishment of an offense or crime.

WREST *v.*
1. To twist or extort by violence; to pull or force from by violent wringing or twisting.
2. To distort; to turn from truth or twist from its natural meaning by violence; to pervert.
3. To take or force from by violence.

WRETCHED *a.*
1. Very miserable; sunk into deep affliction or distress.
2. Calamitous; very afflicting.
3. Worthless; paltry; very poor or mean.
4. Despicable; hatefully vile and contemptible.

WRING *v.*
1. To twist; to turn and strain with violence.
2. To distress; to press with pain.

WROTH *a.*
Very angry; much exasperated.

WROUGHT *v.*
1. Worked; formed by work or labor.
2. Effected; performed;

produced.

3. Used in labor.

4. Formed; fitted.

WRUNG *past tense of wring.*

YE *pron.* (1913)
The plural of the pronoun of the second person in the nominative case.

YEA *adv.*
1. Yes; a word that expresses affirmation or assent.
2. Enforces the sense of something preceding; not only so, but more.
3. Used to denote certainty, consistency, harmony, and stability.

YEARN *v.*
1. To be strained; to be pained or distressed; to suffer.
2. To long; to feel an earnest desire; to have a desire or inclination stretching towards the object or end.

YIELD *v.*
1. To produce, as land, stock or funds; to give in return for labor, or as

profit.
2. To produce, in general.
3. To resign; to give up.

YOKE *n.*
A piece of timber, hollowed or made curving near each end, and fitted with bows for receiving the necks of oxen; by which means two are connected for drawing.

YOKEFELLOW *n.*
1. An associate or companion.
2. A mate; a fellow.

YONDER *a.*
Being at a distance within view.

YONDER *adv.*
At a distance within view.

YOUWARD (Strongs)
You as the object of a verb or preposition.

ZEAL *n.*
Passionate ardor in the pursuit of any thing.

ZEALOUS *a.*
Warmly engaged or ardent in the pursuit of an object.

CPSIA information can be obtained
at www.ICGtesting.com
Printed in the USA
BVHW072253141021
618852BV00002B/29